HAUNTED!

Ghost Stories

from round and about

Stratford, Redditch, Bromsgrove

and Alcester

*

Anne Bradford

*

Illustrations by Nigel Bunegar

Hunt End Books

First Published by Hunt End Books
in June 1992

Graphics by Hurlston Design Ltd. Bournville, Birmingham
Cover by John L Bradford
Printed in Great Britain by BPCC Wheatons Ltd, Exeter

Dedicated to the Ghost of William Avery

No exorciser harm thee!
Nor no witchcraft charm thee!
Ghost unlaid forbear thee!
Nothing ill come near thee!

William Shakespeare (Hamlet)

Acknowledgements

I would first like to thank those who have contributed the ghost stories which make up this collection. I hope they are pleased with the result.

Secondly, this book could not have been written without the help of Ann Jones of Astwood Bank who, despite working on her own book, found time to help me with mine.

Thanks go also to the following: the librarians at Alcester, Stratford and particularly Redditch where the enthusiasm of Philip Davis, the local history librarian, persuaded me to start collecting these ghost stories; Barry Meade, Curator of Forge Mill Museum; Elizabeth Atkins of the Feckenham Historical Society; Hilda Wilkes and John Lewis of the Bordesley Historical Society; and to the Editors of the *Redditch Advertiser, Stratford Herald* and *Feckenham News*. The Editor of the *Redditch Advertiser* has allowed relevant press cuttings to be used.

Mr Aubrey Gwinnett has kindly given me permission to quote from his own book, *The Story of the Angel Inn, Alcester*, and that of his father (Arthur Gwinnet) *A History of Alcester*. Mr H L Gray-Cheape has permitted the use of several pages from *The Squire of Bentley* - the author, Maudie Ellis, was his great aunt. I am indebted to the Marquis of Hertford first for his contribution and secondly for allowing me to quote from the Ragley Hall guide. The proprietors of Salford Hall Hotel, Abbots Salford, sent me their booklet *The Tragic Legend of Salford Hall* with permission to use it freely. The meticulous detail given about the legend is quite impressive.

Finally, on the home front, thanks go to Angela, who not only spread the news among her schoolfriends that I was looking for ghost stories but also kept my house in order while I was working on them. Thank you to my husband who bought me a word processor for Christmas and has hardly seen me since and to my son and daughter who cooked their own meals days after day. Now that the book is at the printers their ghost of a mother will materialise in full. (No groans, please).

Illustrations

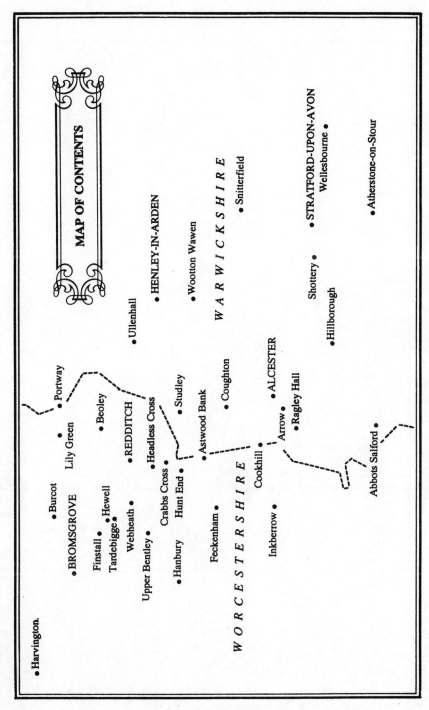

MAP OF CONTENTS

Harvington.

• Burcot

Lily Green

• Portway

• BROMSGROVE

• Beoley

Finstall • • Hewell
Tardebigge •

Webheath •

• REDDITCH

Upper Bentley •

• Crabbs Cross

• Headless Cross

• Hanbury   Hunt End •

• Studley

• Astwood Bank

• Ullenhall

• HENLEY-IN-ARDEN

• Wootton Wawen

W A R W I C K S H I R E

Feckenham •

• Coughton

• Snitterfield

W O R C E S T E R S H I R E

Cookhill •

• ALCESTER

Inkberrow •

Arrow •

• Ragley Hall

Shottery •

• STRATFORD-UPON-AVON

Wellesbourne •

• Hillborough

Abbots Salford •

• Atherstone-on-Stour

vii

Contents

Introduction

When I began collecting these ghost stories I didn't believe in ghosts. Now, having listened to so many strange stories from the most reliable of people, I am not so sure. I can only tell you exactly what I have found and leave you to make up your own mind.

My interest in ghosts is from a purely historical point of view. To understand people of the past, we need to be aware of their attitude towards the paranormal. Until the discoveries of modern science the world seemed to be full of mystery and magic. Life was uncertain. Bad luck could strike at any time without warning and, apparently, without reason. Cattle could fall sick, crops could fail and children could be curiously ill. Imagine also living in this part of the country when the vast dark impenetrable forest of Feckenham stretched for miles and was inhabited by wolves and wild boars. Imagine the darkness of the night relieved only by the glow of an oil lamp or a flickering candle. Drama lurked round every corner. Childbirth, illness and death took place in the home, not the hospitals and were beset by omens, superstitions and curious ceremonies. Shakespeare's plays, not surprisingly, are full of witches, ghosts and fairies. Going further back into history a walk round the outside of the Norman church at Holt Fleet shows how religion, folklore and magic were linked in the medieval mind. There, carved on a Christian building, are mythological birds, snakes, green men and dragons.

How did I come to start this collection? I was doing some research involving local history in the Redditch library when I came across *The William Avery Memorial Volumes* (1823-1906) which contain an interesting collection of ghost stories. Some of them are signed 'J M Woodward' and the picturesque prose surely identifies him as the brilliant amateur archeologist who wrote *The History of Bordesley Abbey* in 1866. I suggested to Mr Davis, the local history librarian, that I thought this was part of the area's heritage and should be updated and published. Mr Davis agreed and said that he needed a register of local hauntings to help with the occasional query from members of the public. For a couple of years I did nothing, hoping someone else would undertake this work; but no-one did.

As soon as I began, two problems arose. First, what area should I cover; and secondly, what exactly is a ghost story? In both cases I have taken the William Avery collection as a guide. Mr Avery used stories from places which, in his day, would have taken twenty or thirty minutes to reach and so I have followed suit. His collection covered all things 'supernatural', one of the most interesting anecdotes, for example, being a remedy for sick cows by a white witch doctor! I therefore embarked on a general survey of all paranormal activity and have included such peculiarities as odours of sanctity and UFOs.

I have noticed an interesting feature: a person who sees one ghost is likely to see a second. Mrs Judge, widow of Rev Nicolas Judge, believed both Hanbury and Beoley vicarages to be haunted and the technical manager of the Palace Theatre has seen both the Palace Theatre ghost and the 'Lady of the Lake' at Hewell Grange. I have wondered whether or not this suggests that some people possess an extrasensory perception - a sensitivity to an extra dimension. I have therefore included narratives from three people who think they might be psychic, a retired lady from Cookhill, a mother from Matchborough and an ex-lorry driver from Batchley. I make no judgement but merely present their stories as food for thought.

I anticipated spending a few weeks compiling a little booklet. I never dreamed that I would be faced with such a wealth of information and its variety and volume have posed many problems. How, for example, could I clearly distinguish bits of gossip from bona fide eye-witness accounts? I decided to arrange the text according to separate sources of information and label each accordingly. The book is presented as a directory of the paranormal. (My son suggested I should call it *The Next Life Directory!*).

The main problem, which far overshadowed any other difficulty, was that of persuading anyone who had seen a ghost to talk about it. I know that some found this such a horrific experience that they simply wanted to forget about it. The majority, I think, were afraid of public opinion. I managed to persuade a few to tell me their stories by promising anonymity and I have spent the last six months acting much like an MI5 agent. I have received and made mysterious telephone calls and I have met other women in gloomy pubs, identified only by a code name!

I hope this book will encourage many other people to come forward with details of ghosts seen or heard. The local history librarians at Redditch, Stratford and Alcester would like to receive a written account of paranormal experiences in their areas which they could keep on record. No doubt readers of the future will be as fascinated by contemporary ghost stories as we are by those in the archives.

ABBOTS SALFORD

Salford Hall

Near Abbots Salford is a large stone Elizabethan house with
unusually-shaped gables. This is Salford Hall, now a hotel, which
bears the date 1602 over the porch but was originally built in the
fifteenth century by the abbots of Evesham. Here it is not only
possible to sleep in a haunted house but also to have a murder
included, for the proprietors organise various holiday activities
including murder weekends.

Salford Hall has been the scenario for one of the most fascinating
ghost stories of all time. From 1807 to 1829 it was occupied by a
community of Benedictine nuns who had been forced to leave
Cambrai because of the French Revolution. They converted the hall
into a girls' boarding school.

In 1815 two sisters, Evra and Wyom Hendon (eleven and
thirteen respectively) were left at the school under mysterious
circumstances together with enough money to complete their
education. The nuns had instructions to look after the girls until
Wyom was eighteen, then to place a curiously worded advertisement
in *The Times*.

The girls were very happy at the school, the nuns treating them
as if they were their own children. On Wyom's eighteenth birthday
the nuns placed the advertisement as they had been instructed and a
letter subsequently arrived telling Wyom to go to a certain house in
London. Goodbyes were said with many tears and promises to write.
Weeks passed but no word came from Wyom. Evra and the nuns
became increasingly concerned. Then Evra began walking in her
sleep. The nuns tried to watch her throughout the night but she
seemed to disappear into thin air. One day, a distressed Evra
confided in the abbess that she had dreamt that her sister was being
held prisoner.

The abbess's fears increased when she discovered that the
address to which Wyom had been called did not exist. The police
were notified and eventually, thanks to the presence of mind of a
young doctor, Wyom was traced to a house in Buckingham where
she was found to be suffering from stab wounds. Her guardian's son,
with an accomplice, had kidnapped her and tried to force her either

to marry him or to sign away her fortune to him. Sadly, by this time, the highly-strung Evra had fallen ill with grief and had died.

Wyom's captor was in a state of hysteria and a curious story emerged. He claimed to have been driven crazy by the ghost of a girl who appeared every night and would not leave him alone.

Wyom recovered fully to marry the young doctor responsible for her rescue and eleven years later a little Miss Wyom Evra Hendon Lapel began school at Salford Hall.

A sixty-page booklet The Tragic Legend of Salford Hall *giving a detailed account of the above story is available from Salford Hall, Abbots Salford, Warwickshire.*

ALCESTER

The Abbey and the Church

Alcester is the place to live for those who dream of finding buried treasure, for it was once a well-to-do Roman town - probably the only town between Cirencester and Lichfield. Finds of coins, bits of pottery and other Roman artefacts are quite common when digging gardens. Occasionally, a really valuable find is made. In 1638 a hoard of 800 pieces of silver was found by Rev Clarke's neighbour when digging a cellar. In 1873 an eleventh century cross was found in the Rector's garden; it is now in the British Museum. No-one knows why Alcester, which was so important in Roman, Saxon and Norman times, almost faded away. Perhaps it was because of two well-known curses which were laid upon the town! The first is said to be by St Chad who became Bishop of Mercia in about 700 AD.

> Alcester was a great place for ironworks even in this early age and large numbers of blacksmiths were employed in them. These men worked in open sheds and one day when St Chad, in the course of his missionary labours, came to preach to them, these men with one accord made such a furious clatter with their hammers that not a syllable of his sermon could be heard. The Saint was obliged at last to leave them.*

The second curse was by the monk, Ansel, and put upon the great Benedictine abbey which once stood to the north of the town, close to where the playing fields of Alcester Grammar School now lie. The Abbey was founded in the twelfth century by King Stephen, in a time of political turmoil and near civil war. He hoped that his generosity would win him the support of the Church, but the King then ruined his image by quarrelling with one of the monks, Ansel, and arranging to have him murdered. Ansel, with his dying breath, cursed the abbey. The curse seems to have been surprisingly effective because the abbey suffered so many disasters that three hundred years later King Henry VI decided to disband the

---

*From A J Gwinnett's A History of Alcester.
Other versions of this legend are in existence. A J Gwinnett states:
    The same story is in effect attributed to St Ecqwyn when preaching on the banks of the Arrow. St Ecqwyn also gave the ironworkers tails!

brotherhood altogether.

Ansel's ghost now decided to put in an appearance in two different places, many miles apart. He visited King Henry and told him that, if the abbey were dissolved, England would lose France (which, of course, it did). Then, later, he appeared to a group of monks in St Nicholas' Church and instructed them to find his bones and bury them in consecrated ground as his curse had been accomplished in full.

At the beginning of this century, another ghost appeared in the church. Mrs Lee was polishing the church plate when the ghost of Sir Fulke Greville, who lies in the church carved in alabaster with his wife, emerged from the shadows, then dissolved.

The church still seems to be haunted, although whether this is by Ansel the monk or Sir Fulke Greville, no-one knows. The Reverend David Cooper Capron, Priest in charge of St Nicholas' writes:

> I've spoken to the Verger... he does state that the bell-ringers (of which he is a member) refer to the sound of ghostly steps coming up the bell tower on practice night from time to time - but they never actually see anything. I understand also from the Verger that on one occasion something brushed past his predecessor in the central aisle - but nobody could be seen.

The Angel Inn

The Angel Inn (now converted into two houses, numbers 4 and 5 Church Street) was once an inn of some renown. It was here that Queen Victoria stayed when she was Princess of Kent; and here where the wedding breakfast of the Prince of Wales and Princess Alexandra of Denmark was celebrated.

The exact date when the Angel Inn began entertaining visitors is not known, but it was a thriving business by the seventeenth century. Perhaps its first guests were pilgrims travelling to the shrine of St Faith in Alcester (now St Nicholas' Church). The inn became important in the stage coach era because of its position on the London to Holyhead road. Many coaches called regularly, among them the London coach which left the Angel at 2 am every Tuesday and arrived in the capital at 9.30 am the following day.

An ancient building with such a lively history is often haunted and, sure enough, a phosphorescent man has been seen here, the ghost, it is believed, of Captain Richard Hill, described as 'a villain to the bone'!

Old Published Reports

The following is an excerpt from *The Story of the Angel Inn, Alcester* by Aubrey Gwinnett. The scene opens in Covent Garden, London.

> The story of this ghostly figure began in the late 17th century. At that time a certain Anne Bracegirdle, an actress or singer at Covent Garden, favoured a humble actor, William Mountford, in preference to other gentlemen of a higher station in life.
>
> This rebuff by Anne Bracegirdle piqued a certain Lord Mohun, and incensed his companion, a Captain Richard Hill ...
>
> After some heavy drinking one night Hill determined to kill Mountford, and whilst the man was held by Lord Mohun, Hill stabbed him several times...

Hill then fled to a moated grange at Moons Moat (near Redditch). One evening in 1693, the local constable happened to be passing the grange when he heard a woman screaming, then the sound of a heavy object being dropped into the moat. He hurried away to get help but by the time he was able to return everything appeared to be normal. However, one female member of the Moon family was never seen again.

Once again Captain Hill fled, this time to the Angel Inn where he assumed the name of Captain Richards. Aubrey Gwinnett continues the story:

> As a "well-mannered, genial and handsome man," Hill soon became friendly with the people of Alcester. One of them - the heir to the old Pumphrey family title - invited him, in January 1693, to a party at the Pumphrey family house near Alcester Town Hall, now called Churchill House.
>
> Captain Hill danced with one of the noted local beauties, Moll Patley, and afterwards went into an adjoining room. Here, after playing cards, he was involved in a quarrel and drew his sword, but he was overpowered. After being put out of the house he went across the road back to the "Angel", vowing vengeance on those with whom he had quarrelled.
>
> Hill was supposed to have left the "Angel" the month after this incident, but a 19th century writer says that he was "strongly inclined" to

think that Hill did not leave the inn at all, and that "his remains still moulder in our midst".

Probably it was about this time that the "Angel" became known as a haunted inn. The landlady then, says this writer, was a Mistress Hancock, "a shrewd, strong-minded woman, well fitted for her position and not likely to be led away by cold fancies". A chambermaid named Clarson who worked for her, however, seems to have been repeatedly frightened at night.

Discovery

In 1937 a suggestive discovery was made at the "Angel". A large, closed oven, bricked up years before when a kitchen was converted into a sitting room, was found to contain a rough oblong box with an anchor burnt into its lid, and two swords underneath it.

Inside the box were the remnants of a military cloak, a low crowned felt hat, some small show buckles, a yellow vest woven with gold, and an empty snuff box.

Also in the oblong box were two almost illegible letters about a loan … Both these letters were addressed to "Captain Richards" …

The discovery of this oblong box was followed by some strange manifestations when the " Angel", which had recently been turned into a private house, was occupied by a family.

The story is continued by a "well known lady in Alcester", who said that she was in bed with her husband when it seemed that a heavy body had fallen across the door, causing the framework to rattle and shake. Her husband closed the door, but the vehement rattling was repeated, again and again.

The lady, now thoroughly afraid, waited with "awful trembling and chilliness at heart" to see the door open to its full extent, and she became conscious that something had entered the room.

She could not describe her "tremor and agony, but wildly stared into vacancy" as she distinctly heard some brass handles of a chest-of-drawers rattle "as if a body had brushed past it". A wardrobe was pushed back against the wall and a chair by the bedside was rocked violently.

"Overhead, following the drapery, came the only sound we heard: a hissing as of one breathing heavily, then a low mocking laugh, enough to curdle one's blood", so the lady's story goes.

After that there was a heavy thud, exactly over the long-concealed oven, then silence.

The lady and her husband were not the only ones to have heard the sounds of the apparition.

An invalid in an adjoining room was repeatedly disturbed by what she said was a "faint sibilation". In the dim light she says that she twice saw a "tremulous mist, oval in shape, gliding along the room until it faded in the recesses".

On another occasion this lady said that she was sitting down when she was conscious of pressing something which yielded like an air cushion and at once a body, or some other object, reformed and brushed past her.

On the cold, dark night of 26th March, 1884, an interested person decided to test for himself the truth of these tales about ghosts, and to brave what he said were the "horrors of a night in the Angel".

He went up to a badly lighted bedroom taking with him as a companion his old and faithful dog which, about one o'clock in the morning, startled him by a "low prolonged growl".

He says that he was then dimly conscious of a "faint luminous centre" which he thought at first came from a night light in the room, but as he realised what it really was he became "tongue-tied with fright".

A sound - "like the wintry wind passing through the withered leaves of oak, ending in a mocking laugh" - was something, he said, he would never forget.

There was a kind of amber phosphorescence revealing the outline in which stood, or rather floated, the image of a man. It wore a long cloak of dark material, and rough, large boots, and the face, said the ghost-hunter - "Ah, the face comes back to me with terrible distinctness".

The hair had been closely cropped, the face was ghastly pale, the eyes were large and luminous, and followed him with "beseeching earnestness".

The man later related that the eyes of his dog had "gleamed like fire" and that it crouched against him as he moved towards the apparition, and pressed even closer to him as he actually touched the wall behind the ghostly presence. He writes that he was conscious of his "passing through an impalpable presence", which repelled him and threw him back, before he saw the spectre re-form. Only then it seemed to be "strangely agitated, passing hither and thither with restless eagerness, and causing a current of air as if fanned by invisible winds".

He managed to ask: "Are you Captain Richard Hill? Are you at rest, and what do you want?" The features of the apparition were strangely contorted at these questions, its eyes shone, and when it was asked, "Will you speak," its small hand, "delicate as that of a woman", was raised to its mouth before it vanished and the man and his dog found themselves alone.

Ghostly Gossip

One night about ten years ago, in one of the old cottages in Butter Street, a young boy had this terrible, realistic nightmare that he could see a lady burning. He particularly remembered that her hair was on fire.

His mother was curious and decided to investigate the history of the building. At first she could find nothing, then she discovered that the part of the house in which the boy had been sleeping originally belonged to the house next door. Further research revealed that during the seventeenth century, a maid had been burned to death there.

The Arrow Mill, Arrow

ARROW

The Arrow Mill

The entrance to the Arrow Mill (once part of the Ragley estate) is across the road from Ragley Hall. The mill, enlarged and developed, is now a hotel, restaurant and public house, set picturesquely on the banks of the river Alne and surrounded by lush meadows.

The Sisam family were tenants of the mill from 1826 to 1921. James Sisam spent his early years there and has since researched its history. He says that there was a mill in existence in 1086 but the present building dates from about 1800. In 1888 Arrow Mill was converted to roller milling instead of millstones as the former produced a whiter flour which was in demand at that time. Water turbines replaced water wheels in the late 1800s; the former were more efficient.

The General Manager, Simon Woodhams, describes not one but three ghosts that haunt the mill.

The river which flows past the mill sometimes runs red. It is said that this is a ghostly reminder of an incident which occurred in the middle of the last century when the miller of Oversley Mill, which is just down the river, beheaded his wife. The head was carried downstream and got stuck in the sluice here. The river was red with blood and since that time it occasionally runs red.

Then we have a woman in grey on the second floor - she is always dressed completely in grey. We were told about this ghost when we first took over the premises. In the 1890s two sisters ran the mill but one of them got caught in the machinery and she is the one who is supposed to haunt the upper floor. They were members of the Sisam family who ran the mill and were tenants here for three generations.

We had someone here only two or three weeks ago who said he felt someone sitting on his bed in the night. I have had past members of staff who claimed to have seen her but none of my present staff have seen her. This may be because the Arrow Mill has been developed into a hotel. The second floor is residential now and there are a number of people wandering about. If the staff did see a grey lady they wouldn't think anything about it.

Our oldest ghost is that of a white buck which roams the grounds surrounding Arrow Mill, pursued by a bodiless head. The head belongs to Thomas Burdett, who was a member of a well-known Warwickshire family who once owned the mill. In 1477 King Edward IV decided to go hunting around Arrow and shot a white buck which was Thomas's pride and joy. Thomas made a few unfortunate remarks about the King which his enemies lost no time in relaying to the King's ears and poor Thomas was beheaded for treason.

Ragley Hall

In the sixth century, the Saxon lady of the manor wore a large golden brooch, a brooch which remained at Ragley for fourteen centuries until it was stolen in 1988.

In 711 the King of Mercia gave Ragley to Evesham Abbey. Seven hundred years later the Abbey sold Ragley to Sir John Rous.

Ragley Hall is a magnificent Palladium house built in 1688 by Robert Hooke, a contemporary of Sir Christopher Wren. Of all the great houses which he designed, only Ragley remains. For over three hundred years the house has been owned by the Seymour family, who counted among its ranks Lady Jane Seymour, Henry VIII's third wife.

The present Marquis of Hertford inherited Ragley Hall at the age of nine and has dedicated his life to restoring the house for the benefit of the general public. He has contributed the following ghost story from about one hundred years ago.

On the A435 about half way between the Ragley Lodge gates in Arrow and Kingley corner, there is a place called the Springs. I think there is still a water trough there. Beside this spring there sometimes stood a little old lady who was apparently in the habit of wanting a lift from any passing carriage to Dunnington Cross Roads, about two miles along the main road to Evesham. On arrival at Dunnington cross roads, the driver would get down to assist the old lady out of the carriage, only to find she was not there.

After a time, and after complaints were being made that the old lady was alarming people, somebody dug around the spring and found the bones of a little old lady. These bones were laid to rest in Arrow Churchyard in the early years of this century, and the little old lady was never seen again.

Friendly phantom creams off the milk

by ANDY PARKES

A THIRSTY ghost is haunting Astwood Bank residents and leaving them with half empty milk bottles.

The friendly phantom has been visiting Eastwood Court since it was first built, in 1990, and can often be heard walking the empty corridors.

As well as hearing mysterious footsteps and feeling unexplained cold draughts residents also say lights are switched on and off and things disappear.

But despite these ghostly goings-on residents are happy to have the uninvited visitor and say she's welcome any time.

Dorothy Burns said: "We think it's a woman and we know she cannot hurt us.

"This building was put up on the site of an old factory and we think she used to work there.

"She was around most over Christmas, every night, at the same time just after midnight, the lift came down from the top floor and the doors would open but it was always empty.

"We felt a cold breeze and there was a strange smell, a bit like perfume".

Another resident, Irene Walker said: "No-one has seen the ghost, but ever since the scheme opened there have been strange happenings, like cold winds and mysterious footsteps.

"Lights have also been switched on and off but the strangest thing of all is that some people have discovered bottles of milk, still sealed but half empty, on the doorsteps".

Most people living in Eastwood Court, Foregate Street, agree that a spirit has moved in but think she is only mischevious and won't do them any harm.

As long as the residents are left enough milk for their morning coffee they seem happy to have friendly ghost around.

Redditch Advertiser, 12 March 1992

ASTWOOD BANK, CRABBS CROSS, HEADLESS CROSS AND HUNT END

If the residents of the higher parts of these villages could take their houses back in time eight thousand years or so, they would open their front doors to find groups of nomadic man wandering past, or herds of bison or wild deer. For the Evesham Road and the Ridgeway were part of a prehistoric ridgeway running along the western edge of the Arrow valley. It would have been as wide as the ridge allowed and comprised dozens of narrow tracks roughly parallel but constantly intermingling and diverging.

Known locally as 'the old part of Redditch', with justification, it provides some mysterious tales.

Astwood Bank

Do ghosts need to visit the small room? A family in Astwood Bank has some kind of manifestation which has made use of their facilities. The mother of the family describes their ghostly resident.

> I'm sure our house is haunted. There are curious footsteps at night time and inexplicable bumps and thuds. Articles mysteriously disappear and turn up later in an unusual place; a few weeks ago I lost a valuable pen from off the kitchen table then this week I felt something under my feet and there was the pen rolling on the floor. Jewelry is another favourite item for the ghost to hide, my earrings are always going missing.
>
> My husband scoffs at the idea of a ghost but yesterday evening when he decided to change his trousers, he took them off, put the belt on the bed, pulled on another pair of trousers - and the belt had disappeared. The bed has been stripped but the belt has not been found.
>
> Every day something weird happens. This morning I had definitely turned off the dishwasher but when I went into the kitchen a couple of hours later the dishwasher was turned on and working.
>
> One evening, four years ago, my daughter was sitting with her boyfriend in the living room when they both heard the ghost pay a visit to the downstairs small room. Footsteps crossed the hall, the bathroom door opened and the light was switched on, then they heard the cistern

handle squeak. The light went off, the bathroom door opened and footsteps approached. My daughter opened the living room door to see who was there, but the house was empty.

Ghosts are generally thought to be the spirits of the deceased but this is not necessarily so. Over recent years there has been a great deal of interest in the case of a schoolmaster on the continent who was often seen by his pupils in two places at once. He once separated into two people while standing in front of his class.

Ann Jones, of Astwood Bank, provides an anecdote about the ghost of a living person.

Twenty-five years ago a close friend of mine, Betty, emigrated to Australia but we have kept in touch over the years. Then in 1989, Betty was asked to speak at a meeting for the first time and was, of course, very nervous and apprehensive. I thought about her a lot and one night I dreamed that I was sitting on the back row listening to Betty and smiling encouragement. Imagine my surprise when, a few days later, I received a letter from Betty saying that she had looked up while she was speaking and seen me sitting at the rear of the hall. She said that I had looked up and smiled at her. The time that Betty saw me in the hall and the time of my dream was, as far as we could make out from further correspondence, the same.

Crabbs Cross, Evesham Road

Young people in their early teens seem to have a particular sensitivity to the paranormal. This young lady was thirteen when she saw her ghost.

About three years ago I came home from school and found that everyone had gone out and the house was empty. I sat down in the living room and suddenly saw this shadowy vision of a woman wearing a black skirt to her ankles and a checked blouse with a long collar, looking downwards slightly and opening and shutting her right hand. The experience lasted for about 30 seconds, then the shadow faded slowly. I just thought I was seeing things.

Later, when I told my parents we talked about the history of our house, which was built in the late 1800s. They happened to mention that, until they bought the house in 1960, it had been a hairdresser's, for how long they did not know. I suddenly realised that this was what the woman was doing, she was cutting someone's hair with an invisible pair

14

of scissors, although no-one was there.

Many people have asked me if I am certain about the costume because women did not wear long black skirts for most of this century, but this is definitely what I saw.

Headless Cross, Feckenham Road

Ghostly Gossip

Down Feckenham Road is a block of flats which has been built on the site of an old factory. There was one part of the factory which no-one would go into alone or at night because it had a reputation for being haunted. Now the occupants of one of the flats complain that doors are mysteriously locked or unlocked during the night and that, while they sit in the evenings, something brushes past, touching their hair.

Hunt End, Love Lyne

A curious little anecdote which dates back to the 1970s and is told by Denzil Ernest Dedicoat, a landscape gardener.

There is a house in Love Lyne with a yew tree in the garden, I was working there about twenty years ago. One day, I went round the back of the house and suddenly this feeling hit me that someone else was there although I was working alone and I knew that the place should have been empty.

The sensation was so strong that I looked through a window on the side of the house and to my surprise saw a family of four eating a meal at a polished table. There was a father, mother and two adolescent children, the table was very well laid out with a great deal of cutlery and plenty of food. I didn't stare because I thought they were real, but I had the impression that they were a well-mannered family. I didn't have time to look at their clothes but they seemed to be wearing mostly browns. It was only the next day I found out that the house had definitely been empty.

In the same house a young electrician was sitting at the top of the stairs eating his lunch and his tool kit suddenly flew down the stairs. He would never go back into the house again.

BROMSGROVE

The market town of Bromsgrove lies between Redditch and Kidderminster. Once described as a 'large and dirty place, full of shops and manufacturers of nails, needles and some ... coarse linens", it is now clean, spacious and liesurely. In the centre of the town stands a statue of one of its most famous sons, the poet A E Housman, author of *The Shropshire Lad*.

The coat-of-arms of Bromsgrove Council includes the head of a boar. A local legend associates it with Sir Ryalas, an imaginary figure, who loved hunting. He was out riding one day when he came across a distraught wild woman who sobbed that her husband and thirty of his men had just been killed by a wild boar. Sir Ryalas rose to the challenge and blew his horn to all four points of the compass. The boar emerged from the forests and after a long and bloody battle, the knight managed to kill it. He returned triumphant to the woman, but instead of being pleased she was furious and began clawing him with long, sharp nails. Sir Ryalas recognised her as a witch and split her head in two with his axe. Later, he discovered that she had planned to kill him by transforming her son into a boar, thinking it would gore him to pieces.

Birmingham Road

165A Birmingham Road (known locally as 'the path lab') is now the headquarters of the Bromsgrove & Redditch Health Authority but was originally built, in 1836, as the Bromsgrove Union Workhouse and was used as such until 1901.

I worked there for twelve months during 1986/7 and discovered that the presence of a ghost was so accepted that cleaners were not asked to work outside office hours. One of the cleaners described to me how she arrived at work early one morning and in the semi-darkness opened a cupboard at the top of the stairs to see an elderly gentleman with white hair sitting there. She screamed, banged the cupboard door shut and raced down the stairs to get help. The ghost had, of course, disappeared by the time she returned.

The grim institution brought a great deal of suffering and unhappiness for the poor of the area and there are several candidates for this particular ghost. Neville Land (author of *The*

Victorian Workhouse) writes: 'Supposedly the apparition is that of a male pauper who committed suicide at the workhouse in the last century'.

The following incident happened to me while I was working there. I thought nothing of it at the time and it was not until I began collecting these ghost stories that it occurred to me I could have had a paranormal experience.

Not the sort of person to believe in ghosts, I willingly volunteered to stay until late one winter evening to finish a document required for the following day. I was alone in the building and working in my office on the top floor, only two lights in use, one in my office and the other in the entrance hall. Suddenly, the fire bells rang out for a few seconds, then stopped. I continued working. Ten minutes later it happened again. Then a few minutes later, again. And again. Thinking this was someone's idea of a joke I angrily toured the building - but it was dark and empty. I had been working about fifteen minutes when the fire bells rang yet again in exactly the same way. This time I looked around both the building and the grounds. The old Bromsgrove hospital had been pulled down and the new one had not yet been built, so I could easily see that no-one was about. Even the works manager's office was locked up. I worked on until 8 pm, the fire bells ringing intermittently throughout; and by that time I could not wait to get out and into the safety of my car. The next day I tackled the works manager. He was very amused but could offer no rational explanation.

Neville Land comments that 'since the building has been divided by new partitions in the last 2-3 years, the ghost has not re-appeared'. I wonder why.

Burcot

Burcot lies to the north east of Bromsgrove with the main Birmingham/Worcester railway line touching its tip. A Redditch postman has contributed the following story:

> I used to be a keen train spotter. One of my favourite haunts was on the Lickey incline, by bridge 106 near Burcot. I used to wait for the Great Western mail train, which was a steam train in those days, on the Devonian run. Sometimes my wife used to wait with me. On this particular day we were both there. The train travelled past then my wife

suddenly said: 'What's that bloke doing over there?' I looked and saw a man bending over, tightening the nuts up with what was called a snipper. I thought that was strange because spring clips are used these days on the gaps in the line so there's no need to tighten the nuts up. Suddenly, he just 'disappeared'. He didn't look like a ghost, he was quite solid, but there's nowhere he could have gone, there's a sheer drop each side of the line. It really put the wind up my wife!

Finstall

The following cuttings from the Redditch Advertiser tell of an apparition seen three times during December 1990 on the Bromsgrove Highway near Finstall. The second driver saw the ghost quite clearly and described it as a woman in a long cloak.

Although the Bromsgrove Highway is new, when it nears Finstall it runs along the line of the old road. This road would have been well-used for at least 800 years as it ran past Hewell Grange, which belonged to Bordesley Abbey. The first Ordnance Survey map of about 1830 shows clearly that it was a major route.

Why did the ghost suddenly decide to put in an appearance? Was a grave disturbed? Did the vibrations of the roadworks create some kind of dimensional disturbance? Or was it merely, as M Wall suggests in his letter, a reflection of the triangular road signs?

Mrs M Taylor saw her ghost on the other side of Redditch, near Bordesley Garage which is not far from the abbey site. As it was part a series of letters to the *Redditch Advertiser*, it has been included here.

Highway horror from the ghoul

TERRIFIED motorists claim they've been confronted by a ghost on a busy Redditch Highway.

Drivers have been left shaking in terror after seeing a woman step in front of them from out of nowhere - then vanish.

The phantom - always dressed in a long cloak - appears on the Redditch to Bromsgrove Highway near Finstall.

Motorists say they've had to swerve to avoid the figure.

Brian Godwin, of Mickleton Close, Oakenshaw, says his son Nigel saw the apparition.

He said: "He was driving on the Highway early one morning when he saw a figure crossing the outside lane.

"Both Nigel and the driver of the car in front of him braked and swerved."

Another driver, who didn't want to be named, said: "My husband had to break hard after seeing a woman in a long cloak in the road."

● Have you seen the mystery highway spectre? Let us know.

Redditch Advertiser, 5 December 1990

Ghostly sightings

*MORE spooked Advertiser readers say they have come
face-to-face with a phantom on Redditch's roads.*
*Stunned callers have told of their hair-raising experiences
all over town.*
*The latest ghoul appears as a woman near Finstall on
the Bromsgrove Highway.*
*One reader reports seeing a monk standing just yards
from the Finstall hauntings.*
*Reports have come from outside the Foxlydiate Hotel,
near Bordesley Garage and near Tardebigge.*

Redditch Advertiser, 12 December 1990

Another ghost

I READ about people seeing a phantom-like figure.
I too saw a similar figure, only it was in a different place near Bordesley Garage on the Birmingham Road.
It was a tall black long-caped figure walking along. What struck me was that it reminded me of something from a film where they wore these long hooded capes.
It was about 11.45 and had been quite misty in patches, a little eerie.
This figure appeared to be walking along the kerb, the lamp showed it quite clearly as we went past.
I turned back to get a better look and literally gasped for it seemed to have a skeleton face skull grey, in colour like someone wearing a mask.
My husband hadn't noticed anything amiss, as he was concentrating on his driving, and my daughter had been talking to the dog.
I wanted them to go back and see for themselves, but they were highly amused and said it was probably someone dressed up for Halloween playing a practical joke.
I am a Christian so not given to fancy. I don't think I imagined it all.
It would be nice to know if there are many others who have seen the same as myself, just to satisfy my own peace of mind.

Mrs Margaret Taylor
Rowan Road
Batchley Estate

Redditch Advertiser, 12 December 1990

Clue to mystery

I AM WRITING in regard of your front page article (December 5 1990) "Highway horror from the ghoul".

As a twice daily traveller on the Redditch Bromsgrove Highway I may have the answer to this mystery. On the stretch of road mentioned near Finstall there are roadworks and triangular roadsigns in the central reservation and as you approach these signs a poor light or fog they appear to move across the road in front of you especially if another vehicle is coming the other way.

This has happened to me on a few occasions and it does give you a shock the first time you see it with the triangular shape of the signs looking like someone in a cloak.

This is my explanation for these ghostly sightings but of course I may be completely wrong and this stretch of road could indeed be haunted by the "woman in the long cloak".

M Wall
Exhall Close
Church Hill South

Redditch Advertiser,
19 December 1990

Mystery spectre

I FEEL I should write in support of the 'mystery spectre' observed on the Bromsgrove Highway.

Our experience a friend and myself were driving towards Redditch on Saturday November 24 at around 12.30 at night.

Near Finstall we became aware of something crossing the path of the car, my friend who was driving braked, unsure of what it was, or what to do. It was unnerving for a few seconds, but disappeared as quickly as it came. We could not identify anything in particular in the dark.

Hilary Lennox
Guinness Close
Headless Cross

Redditch Advertiser,
26 December 1990

Hewell Grange was once one of the many granges owned by Bordesley Abbey. In 1542, Henry VIII paid a visit to Lord Windsor and, surprisingly, announced that he wished to exchange the thriving Windsor domain for Bordesley Abbey and its estates. Lord Windsor protested strongly but it was obvious that if he wanted to keep his head on his shoulders he would have to comply with the King's request. He arrived with his entourage on a wet November afternoon and found the Abbey ruinous and uninhabitable. Understandably, he decided to settle at Hewell Grange.

This was unfortunate for Lord Windsor, particularly as his residence was stocked up ready for Christmas; but it was a stroke of luck for Redditch. He took an interest in local skills, crafts and trades, the local villages flourished and he laid the foundations for the expansion of the needle industry which made Redditch so famous in later years.

Hewell Grange is reputed to be haunted by 'The Lady of the Lake'. Arthur Bunegar, Technical Manager of the Palace Theatre, saw her one chilly November evening, just as it was growing dark.

> When I was a kid I lived down at Batchley and my friends and I, a gang of about half-a-dozen, used to go and play in the ruins of Hewell Grange. I can't tell you what a splendid house and garden it was and it is a great pity that it has been taken over by HM Prisons.
>
> One November evening when we were about ten or eleven years old we went chestnutting there. The evening was cold but a bright moon made everything clear as day. Suddenly, only a few yards away, we saw this lady rise slowly from the lake. She was wearing a huge voluminous dress like a ballroom gown and was all white from head to toe. I had the impression that she was covered by a cloak, the hood of which hid her hair and most of her face but I caught a glimpse of her profile (we saw her from the side) and would guess that she was in her early twenties. She was of average height and quite slim. She was walking towards the derelict ballroom and her dress flowed and fluttered as she moved. She looked quite solid - as real as you or me.
>
> We were terrified. She disappeared and we did too, we just ran for home.
>
> I have since heard the story that the 'Lady of the Lake' was having an affair with a certain fellow and used to meet him by the lake. Her husband or boyfriend found out and murdered her in the middle of the

ballroom. It has never been possible to erase the blood stains from the marble floor. Local tradition says that they only way to get rid of the stain is for someone to live as a hermit for ten years in a nearby cave.

Part of Hewell has a rock face and my friends and I hunted for the cave for years but we never found it.

Tardebigge

The elegant church which crowns Tardebigge hill is a landmark for several miles around Bromsgrove and Redditch. At the foot of the hill the Tardebigge canal is a masterpiece of Victorian engineering.

About a thousand years ago Tardebigge was a parish on the edge of Feckenham forest, becoming large enough to include Bordesley Abbey and, later, Redditch. In the twelfth century King Henry II took a liking to the area and annexed much of it to his forest including the grounds of Hewell Grange and Bordesley Abbey.

Lord Windsor came to live at Hewell Grange in Tardebigge in 1542 and his descendants built what is now the Tardebigge public house as a village hall in 1911. Unfortunately, the villagers were not able to enjoy this gift for long, as it was used as a hospital during the First World War, then sold to Ansell's Brewery in 1946 as part of the family estate, to offset heavy taxation and death duties.

Six years ago the Tardebigge was closed for two years for extensive alterations, reopening in March 1988 with Mr Gerard Ludden as Manager. He was amused when he heard that the pub was supposed to have a ghost.

> The children came home from school crying because they had been told that their new home was haunted. I asked them how the other children could know if they didn't live here. To be honest, I didn't think twice about it; I was much too busy to bother about rumours of a ghost. But I must confess, when we first opened, curious little incidents kept happening. For example, we had a problem with the burglar alarm which kept going off for absolutely no reason. It still goes off now every couple of months and no-one has any idea why. Then there was this strange sensation which I felt whenever I walked across the *function room from the false door to the other side. It's difficult to describe - it was a kind of chill in the air which made me shudder although I wasn't physically cold.

---

* *The Tardebigge has a short wing projecting backwards from each end, the southern one used for weddings and large parties. The left-hand wall is blank on the inside but in the same place on the outside wall is a door*

From time to time we have guests who claim to be psychic and they tell me we have a ghost here. A couple of years ago a lady who had heard that the place was haunted asked if she could have a look round to try to locate the ghost. She assured us we do have a 'presence' named Emily who was once a nurse here but that she is a kind ghost and there is no need to be afraid of her. She walks between the false doors of the function room and the opposite wall and when I was talking to my staff afterwards I discovered that most of our weird experiences had happened in that area. I was very surprised and it really made me think!

Strange to say, since our guest discovered a little more about the ghost I have not felt the sudden chill in the function room. Instead, I now get a strange feeling of peace and tranquillity. You might think, since the function room is supposed to be haunted, I would be afraid to go in there. Not a bit of it: I go in every evening and never even bother to switch the lights on.

The feeling that there is someone with me is so strong that as I come out I always say, 'Goodnight Em!'

Two of Mr Ludden's staff have strange tales to tell. Barbara, his Assistant Manager, has worked at the Tardebigge since 1988.

When we first opened something very unusual happened. The top shelf of the bar is full of two-pint tankards, and just on that day they kept splitting down the middle. We could see them shattering before our eyes, with no-one anywhere near them. There was no regular pattern: sometimes two would split together, sometimes three. Sometimes we would go an hour or even two without a breakage: then another time there would only be a ten-minute interval. It was very weird. These tankards have thick bases, you can drop them on the floor and they don't break. Yet they were shattering for no apparent reason.

One of my tasks is to write out the table plans for large functions. I was doing this one lovely sunny afternoon in June last year, kneeling on the floor just in front of the false doors. The sun was streaming in through the windows and the atmosphere was not at all eerie. Suddenly, I felt someone come up behind me, then I felt a tap on my shoulder. I'm saying 'tap' but really it was more like a firm poke. I turned round to see who it was, and to my surprise no-one was there.

Just over two years ago we had a great strapping bloke, John, working behind the bar. He was at least six feet six inches tall. One day, he came up from the cellar looking ashen. He said he had heard someone sneezing down there but when he went to see who it was the cellar was empty.

We have problems with our names being called. A young lady's voice comes from behind a dumb waiter which we keep just in front of the false doors. I've only heard it twice because I don't usually work in the function room but the waitresses often hear it. We have a function nearly every Saturday and they hear it at about half of these. Two girls here last year, Samantha and Debbie, found it a real nuisance. They kept saying to each other, 'What do you want?' and 'Did you call me?' and getting very confused.

Pauline is the Restaurant Supervisor at the Tardebigge. Her narrative comes as a surprise because, instead of describing the hauntings of the first ghost, she complains about a second one!

Emily does not seem to have manifested herself very much recently, in fact she seems to have faded away over the past twelve months. Instead, I am having problems in the main lounge. To the right of the main doors (as you come in) is a raised area which I tidy round and dust each morning. For several weeks during the spring of 1991 I kept putting my duster down, then when I turned round to get it the duster had moved, sometimes quite a distance, for example to another chair or table. At first I thought I was being absent-minded but it happened so often that I knew it could not be me all the time. Then early one morning, at about nine o'clock, I was hoovering round when I heard this fella laughing just behind me. I switched off the vaccuum and turned round to see who it was but no-one was there. However, the liquid polish had been knocked over and was trickling across the table although I hadn't been anywhere near it. I told the other staff but I knew from the look on their faces that they thought I was inventing an excuse for knocking the polish over. I found the incident so weird that I refused to go into the raised area early each morning until several staff had arrived.

A few months later a cleaner, Rose, was engaged to take over all this kind of work and exactly the same thing happened to her. First of all her dusters kept moving around, then she heard this bloke laugh behind her - no-one was there but the liquid polish had been knocked over. She left after a week.

A couple of long-term customers live across the road and they say that about twenty years ago, one of our regulars had a passion for practical jokes and, before he died, he spent all his time playing jokes on people. Several times recently they are certain that they have seen him sitting in the raised area.

COOKHILL

Well-known throughout Redditch, this senior citizen whose story appears below, was the wife of a prominent businessman while she herself was a founder member of several popular societies. However, during all these years in the public eye she has carried with her a guilty secret - not a lover, not a bad debt, not a skeleton in the family cupboard, but the fact that she believes she has 'second sight'.

I have the gift of second sight or whatever you like to call it. But I don't like it, I don't want it, I will have nothing at all to do with it and only a few close friends know that I have this. My mother was the same. We could often foretell national disasters by a feeling of dread and difficulty in breathing. We could both sense people coming and surprised people by being at the door to greet them. My daughter has the gift, too, but I tell her to put it aside and have nothing to do with it. If you are highly strung, as I know she is, it can push you over the edge.

I can feel when a person is going to meet with some disaster. I remember one time particularly when I was introduced to an elderly man at Kings Coughton. As I shook his hand I felt cold all over and I couldn't wait to get out of the house. Later, his daughter went to live with him and during this time he died from natural causes. However, she continued to draw his pension and I suppose she wanted to dispose of his body. So she hacked his head off, which was found in a pool, and tried to burn his body.

The first experience of second sight which I can remember was at ten or eleven years of age, when I had a sort of dream or fantasy that I could see my older brother, who was at the battlefront, lying in a field with grass round him. I remember wondering what he was doing and why he was lying like that. The next day we heard that he had been killed in action.

I have seen a few ghosts, always before a death. Our family usually sees a black dog as a death token. If it's a more distant relative, like a cousin, we only see the dog in a flash every now and then. If it's a close relative, it's almost as if a strange dog has moved in with us. I remember when another brother was very ill; we had a black dog ourselves who was only allowed in the kitchen. I was sitting in the lounge and I saw a black dog come in and sit down by the fire. I called out to my husband 'That damn dog's in here again!'. I was amazed when I went out into the kitchen and our own dog was still there. I saw the phantom dog two or three times that day and my brother died that night. I remember the day before I was sitting in my lounge, doing some knitting, when I looked up and saw dark shadows outside the window. I thought, 'What are all those people doing in my garden?' I went outside to look, but no-one was there.

When I was about thirteen I was coming home from confirmation classes with a friend, along a country lane, and we were larking about with my bike. Both of us were riding it, she at the front and I balancing on the saddle. Suddenly, a luminous light rose very slowly from the ground in front of us, moved over the hedge and soared away. It was about eighteen inches wide and had a long tail like a meteor trailing at the back. I shall always remember that. My friend and I screamed and ran for home as fast as our legs would carry us. Our families said it might have been an owl. Apparently at times they can look luminous. Perhaps this was so; but the next week we both had a death in our families. My friend's mother died and my uncle died.

COUGHTON

The main road from Studley to Alcester which passes through Coughton, the A435, was once part of the Roman Icknield Street. The locals speak of a coach and four or six white horses which has been seen in past years going straight across the A435 and into the drive of Coughton Court.

Tom Maries, a retired businessman in Astwood Bank, and President of the Bordesley Society, had a curious experience on that section of road.

> I'm not the sort of person to believe in ghosts. I can only tell you exactly what I saw and let you make up your own mind.
>
> One foggy November evening I was driving home from the Stratford Theatre when, passing through the village of Coughton towards Redditch along the A435 Icknield Street, my headlights picked out a white luminous form, like a human form, about six feet tall and lean with indistinct features. It crossed from the left towards Coughton Court. I stopped my car and my friend and I alighted, and noticed that two cars which were coming towards us had also stopped and the occupants had also alighted. Then we all joined in conversation and confirmed that an apparition had indeed passed over towards Coughton Court.

It seemed at first that it would not be possible to include Coughton Court itself in this collection of ghost stories.

Mrs Marian Buchanan, the National Trust Administrator for Coughton Court, wrote saying: 'I feel this reply is rather negative but we do not really have any proof of experience of ghosts at Coughton Court'. She went on to say that a popular story about the ghost of a grey lady has to be discounted because the geography of the house does not coincide with the description of the route taken by her. In addition, stories of another ghost associated with a sword discovered below the floorboards of the turret in the Tower Room should also be disregarded as there are documents to prove that the sword was given to the Throckmorton family by a friend.

It seemed a pity that this ancient house had no record of a ghostly visitor! It is one of the few houses in this country still occupied by the family who first built it, in this case the Throckmortons who remained staunchly Catholic despite religious persecution.

The house is famous as the place in which the wives of the friends of Guy Fawkes waited to hear the result of the Gunpowder Plot. Less well known is the fact that the Throckmortons were at the head of a plot to depose Elizabeth I and put Mary Queen of Scots on the throne; and in 1688, just when it had been rebuilt following the ravages of the Civil War, the Court was attacked again, this time by an anti-Catholic mob from Alcester. It was therefore very satisfying to read in the Records Office at Stratford that in the late eighteenth century Sir Robert Throckmorton was much troubled by a ghost, and made persistent efforts to get rid of it. Although the information was very brief it did at least provide a spectre for the house.

FECKENHAM

This tiny village gave its name to the vast forest of Feckenham. A manor house which once stood here was used as a hunting lodge by the rich and influential throughout the land; and there was a prison here, too, used for those who transgressed the harsh laws of the forest. All that remains of this is a ditch in a green field.

John of Feckenham was the son of a poor woodcutter who rose to fame and honour in the sixteenth century. He entered a monastery, adopted the name of his birthplace and eventually became the last of Westminster's abbots. He stood on the scaffold with Lady Jane Grey, begging her to renounce her faith, and he heard the dying confessions of Mary I. Unfortunately, the wranglings of the church resulted in him spending the last years of his life in and out of the tower and he died a prisoner at Wisbech Castle in Cambridgeshire.

Feckenham still has the enchanted air of an old town, with Georgian houses lining the main street and a tiny village green which is the site each June of the ancient Feckenham Wake, now called the Feckenham Festival.

The old field names reveal a Feckenham which was haunted in the past by spirits, ghosts and fairies. On the Tithe Award map of 1841 are two fields on the side of the Mount known respectively as Upper and Lower Puck Close; pucks were the mischievous, friendly fairies of English folklore. To the North East of Feckenham Village was a field known as 'Sperrity Pit' which contained an enormous hole surrounded by oak trees. The *Birmingham Weekly Post* of 21 December 1889 reports:

> The pit has been filled up but the trees remain in a small circle to mark its site. There are some traditions of a supernatural character associated with this old pit. Whether it was, in superstitious times, the resort of "spirits from the vasty deep" seen from time to time as they "revisited the glimpses of the moon", or whether the ancient ceremony of "laying departed spirits" which had become troublesome ever occurred at this pit, Nash ... does not inform us.

Astwood Court

Astwood Court lies about a mile to the north-east of Feckenham. Although most of the half timbering was replaced some 200 years ago when it was rebuilt of brick, it remains a fine example of a medieval moated farmhouse. In its early days a drawbridge would have been lowered across the moat during the day, then drawn up at night.

In Feckenham Church is a memorial dated 1604 to the only son and heir of Sir Martin Culpepper. He died tragically at the age of 25 and his early death brought to an end the generations of Culpeppers who had lived at Astwood Court. The first Culpepper seems to have been a strange character. He was an astrologer, a magician and a herbalist. He was probably the author of one of the great reference books of his time known as the *Herbal*, on the properties of herbs and the treatment of disease. Many unusual herbs could, until recently, be found in the field next to Astwood Court.

Strange legends developed around him. He was described in the *Birmingham Weekly Post* of 9 October 1880, as having indulged in

> the magical practice of invoking spirits at the Court (not spirits of the departed dead ... but "spirits of the planets", a distinction fully appreciated by magicians), and it is said that on one occasion, when he was in the "Circle", a spirit presented itself in the form of a ferocious lion or tiger, and struck a table standing near, and that a mark where it was struck ever after remained upon it.

The Victorian historian, W Noakes, also refers to the table but gives another explanation.

> An old oak table ... bore ... the impress of the fingers of a lady ghost, who, probably tired of appearing to no purpose, at last struck the table in a rage and vanished for ever'.

The table was removed in 1816.

In the next field but one to Astwood Court (travelling in the direction of Feckenham) was once a cloven pear tree, mentioned in a survey of the estate at the end of the seventeenth century. On moonlit nights, according to tradition, a ghost walks from the house to the tree. Perhaps this is the spirit of John Culpepper who is said to have been interred beneath the floor of the hall.

Close Encounters

Shaun Pulley, now retired and living near Redditch centre, has a tale to tell about Astwood Court.

From 1939 to 1941 Jack, Bill and Betty Honeybourne were living at Astwood Court. Although Bill was six years or so older than me, we were great friends for about 30 years. In 1939 I went to stay at Astwood Court to help in the dairy for the grand wages of sixpence a week. I remember the house well, particularly the name of John Culpepper carved into the woodwork. Anyway, this one day Bill had a bilious attack which steadily became worse and as we were getting ready for bed he had to rush down the cellar to be sick.

In those days, there was no indoor plumbing and if you had to throw up in a hurry the cellar was the best place. He came rushing back up the stairs, jumped into bed and pulled the blankets over his head. He was a great strapping lad of about nineteen, but he was quivering like a jelly. He told me that he had seen a ghost in the cellar. It was a very, very old lady with a pale face, black cloak, grey hair and a long dress. The curious thing was that ghosts are supposed to be silent but this one wasn't, it was making a rattling noise like a box of matchsticks being shaken.

Hanbury Church

HANBURY

We know that Hanbury dates back to Anglo-Saxon times simply because of its name which is Saxon for 'high town'. It ancient church is set on a hill and it was once necessary to climb 180 steps to its doors, a great trial for coffin bearers. A thousand years ago there was a monastery at Hanbury but this has long disappeared.

Since records began the beauty of Hanbury has been recognised. In early medieval times the Bishops of Worcester selected the site for a park of 130 acres which, three centuries later, Queen Elizabeth I evidently admired because she 'appropriated' it, eventually giving it to Sir Thomas Leighton. In the seventeenth century it was described as 'A stately seate meete for a kinge's pallace'.

In Hanbury church are a series of monuments to the Vernons, a distinguished legal family. Thomas Vernon, who built Hanbury Hall in 1710, is shown in his lawyer's robes and wig. One of the glories of this lovely house is the staircase, painted by Thornhill who also decorated parts of St Pauls Cathedral.

Transport has played an important part in the history of Hanbury. The main road from Droitwich to Alcester runs through the parish and meets the main route from Bromsgrove to Alcester. A saltway once touched its southern edge whilst to the west ran the Worcester and Birmingham Canal alongside the Birmingham and Gloucester railway.

Hanbury Church

Mrs Judge says that during the early 1970's, when her husband was Rector of Hanbury, one of their parishioners had a fright. She was arranging flowers at the eastern end of the church one Saturday morning, when suddenly she heard this noise like a great 'whoosh' near the west door. She later described it as sounding rather like 'a mighty rushing wind'! She nearly dropped her flowers with fright. She stood there for a few moments, unable to move, then she gingerly went to inspect the west door. It was closed tightly. There was no natural way in which the noise could have been made.

Hanbury Vicarage

Rev Nicolas Judge was Vicar of Beoley for 14 years then Rector of Hanbury for 10 years. Mrs Judge tells the story of the haunted vicarage in Hanbury.

My husband and I both felt that Hanbury vicarage was haunted. On one occasion I woke up in the night and felt a terrible sense of evil - it was so bad that I felt that I was going to be swept away by it. I have a friend who has had the same experience.

We had to have a very much loved spaniel put to sleep while we were at The Old Rectory; shortly afterwards the whole family heard the sound of her footsteps coming up the long hall there.

There was one incident I remember in particular. My husband was very interested in collecting antiques, especially silver, and he used to go round to various villages giving talks on the subject. One of our parishioners asked him if he would go to talk to a group at the Swan Theatre and said she would come and fetch us in her car.

My husband had a long, narrow wicker basket with two handles bent over the top. On the top of the basket and wedged between the two handles we put a wooden truncheon, the type that special village constables used to carry. Someone from the parish had let him borrow it.

I put the basket behind the driver's seat and I remember seeing the truncheon firmly stuck between the handles. When we got to the Swan my husband said 'Where's the truncheon?' We looked everywhere, under the seat, on the seat, on the pavement in case it had fallen out; but it had disappeared completely and we have never seen it from that moment to this. It was definitely there in the car when we started off.

The driver had her car almost taken to pieces to try and find it; she felt guilty about my husband losing it, but it was never found.

The Rev Judge was much loved and respected in the community and everyone who knew him felt a sense of loss when he died suddenly just before his retirement. Mrs Judge recalls a curious incident which occurred at this time.

When my husband died it was a terrible shock. I missed him so much.

He used to talk a lot about something called the 'odour of sanctity'. One day, shortly after he died, I came back from my daughter's and ran up to the bathroom. The whole room smelt of violets. It was very strong. I thought I must have knocked over some perfume or something but everything was intact. Then all that he had said about 'the odour of sanctity' came back to me and I thought 'I'm going to test this'. I went into my bedroom for a few minutes and shut the door. When I returned to the bathroom the smell had completely gone.

The Odour of Sanctity

Almost as old as Christianity itself is the tradition of associating saints with an inexplicable fragrance, particularly after death. Legends about the corpses of saints which do not decompose and which produce a wonderful fragrance are well known. Sir Thomas Malory wrote in *Le Morte D'Arthur* that there was 'the sweetest savour that ever man smelt' from the corpse of noble Sir Launcelot

Shakespeare was drawing on the same tradition when, after Ophelia's suicide, Laertes says:

> *Lay her i' the earth*
> *and from her fair and unpolluted flesh*
> *May violets spring!*

The odour of sanctity can be any one of a variety of perfumes; both known, such as lavender, violet or rose, and unknown, yet indescribably beautiful and bringing a sense of well-being to those who inhale it. It is certainly mysterious, having been described as filling only a certain area of a building, assuming various shapes, filling a particular room, ascending in a column, or encircling an object.

A booklet Odour of Sanctity *is available from Mrs E M Case of Red Rock, Brampford Speke, Exeter, Devon.*

HARVINGTON,

Harvington Hall, near Chaddesley Corbett

Harvington Hall is set in peaceful Worcestershire countryside, the old Elizabethan brick walls rising out of a picturesque moat as the building first comes into view.

This is one of the few stately homes which even quite small children can enjoy because it contains a rabbit warren of priests' hiding holes. They were built by John Pakington in the seventeenth century to house Roman Catholic priests who were being persecuted under the strict laws of the day. (A Franciscan monk was caught at nearby Rushock Court and executed at Worcester). It is claimed that this house contains more hiding holes than any other in England.

Harvington Hall is also well-known for the wall paintings discovered beneath layers of whitewash, most of them Elizabethan but some dating back to the end of the fifteenth century.

Alan Cox, the Custodian, recalls two ghostly incidents which have occurred:

> You will appreciate that a house like this lends itself to people claiming to have experienced something weird, for example, inexplicable changes in temperature and a sense of being watched. Since we arrived here as custodians five years ago neither myself nor my wife has ever experienced anything unusual in the house. Stories related to us however have included the following:
>
> In 1987 a lady having a cup of tea in the tearoom before going around the rest of the house insisted that she had seen 'an elderly man in old-fashioned clothes smoking a pipe and looking out of the restaurant window'. She apparently assumed he was a guide in costume having a tea break. We informed her that there was nobody of that appearance in the house, and she later identified the man, from a pen drawing in one of the rooms of the hall, as John Kemble, a Catholic priest executed in 1679, but known particularly because of his 'last request' to smoke a pipe with his gaolers!
>
> In 1988, a visitor to the hall on entering one of the bedrooms said she saw a 'lady in Edwardian dress sitting in the corner of the room'. The room she entered was occupied, in the early years of this century, by a schoolmistress who taught in the village school at the end of the garden.
>
> These are the only two incidents which spring immediately to my mind. My wife and I suspect we are not of a disposition to notice a ghost if we fell over it (or should I say 'walked through it'?).

HENLEY-IN-ARDEN
AND BEAUDESERT

Henley is one long street of ancient buildings. There is no other village in the county which has such an unbroken stretch of historic development. Once an important market town, it lay in the heart of the forest of Arden, where wolves, boars and other wild animals roamed freely.

The first ghost story features The Mount in Beaudesert, an interesting little area often missed by visitors. The road leading to it is quite tiny and obscure, running at right angles from St John's Church in the centre of Henley to St Nicholas' Church which is one of the oldest and prettiest churches in the county. To the east lies a small hill, The Mount, all that is left of one of the castles belonging to the great medieval baron, Simon de Montfort. Although he and his son were killed in the battle of Evesham in 1265, the principles for which he fought survived to set the country on the slow road to parliamentary democracy.

The Mount

A retired Vicar tells this anecdote which occurred while he was the incumbent at Henley.

I once had a letter from a young courting couple who lived on the outskirts of Birmingham. The couple had come to Henley for the day and had gone up on to the Mount, where the castle used to be. They wrote to tell me they had had an unusual experience, for while up there they had seen a lady dressed in old-fashioned costume beckoning to them. She said to the young man: 'This girl is not for you, do not marry her'. Then she faded away.

After this the young couple were uncertain as to whether they should get married or not and they wanted to know if I knew of anyone else who had had a similar experience in that area. I had to acknowledge that I didn't but invited them, if they felt they had a problem, to come and see me and discuss it. But I never heard from them.

The White Swan (Public House and Hotel)

The White Swan is one of the oldest buildings in Henley, dating back to 1358. Stage coaches once pulled in here on the long journey from Birmingham to London. Unfortunately, it was 'modernised' in the seventeenth century by having a false front fitted.

When Jacky Bollard first came to the White Swan the locals warned her that it was haunted by a grey lady. However, the following incident is the only one to occur during her six years as manager.

In the late spring of 1989 we had a party of six adults. Two of them, husband and wife, stayed in room 17. During the night they were woken up by a violent tugging at the quilt. It was rather a sitcom situation, with the wife thinking it was the husband and the husband thinking it was the wife and it was some minutes before they woke up sufficiently to realise that neither of them was pulling the quilt and it was jerking of its own accord. Alarmed, they sat up in bed and saw, moving about the room, dark misty shadows of half-a-dozen people which faded away after a few seconds. The husband took this more calmly than the wife and eventually dropped off to sleep but the wife, who was terrified, remained awake, watching. It was then that she saw the grey lady. She described it to me later as the pale face of a young woman staring out from quite a bulky body which was just a mass of dark grey. She thought the ghost might have looked shapeless because she was wearing a cloak. Like the shadows, the grey lady soon faded.

The locals say that this is the ghost of a maid who once worked here and lived on the top floor. She was having an affair with one of the local gentry and the two used to meet in her room. One night they had a disagreement (rumour has it that he was trying to end the relationship); things became very heated and she was pushed down the stairs, dying from her injuries.

The Gables

The Gables dates back to 1490. It was probably a hospice for the poor and the sick, and a shelter for travellers. It belonged to the Guild of St John the Baptist (the Guild Hall, in the centre of Henley, was built in 1490); but later someone took what remained of the hospice, restored it and made a dwelling house. The front gables date back to the early 1800s but a great block of the wall and much of the house is original.

The Gables, Henley-in-Arden

40

The house now belongs to Mrs Barnsby's sister, Miss Elizabeth Mercer, who is at present in a nursing home. The Rev J Barnsby lives there with his wife and tells the story of the 'lavender lady'.

In the late 1930s or early 1940s, Betty, who is a very sensible woman - she was a Red Cross commandant in her hey-day and later the local librarian - was dusting the stairs, in broad daylight, when a lady came out of the little room on the left, just down from the top of the stairs, went up the three stairs and along the landing. She was wearing an old-fashioned lavender-coloured dress. Betty was just about to call out, 'Hey, what are you doing in my house' when the lady disappeared through the wall.

From 1982 to 1986 my mother-in-law lived with us and she had that little room as a bedsit. In about 1984, one hot summer night, she said, 'I'm going to leave my bedroom door open, it gets so hot'. About 4 am Betty heard her say 'I'm feeling rather cold, I'm going to close the door now. Goodnight'. She explained later that she had said this to my wife, who was standing on the stairs - but my wife had not got out of bed that night, and nor had Betty. My mother-in-law must have seen the 'lavender lady' (as we call her) and thought it was my wife in her nightdress.

However, my wife and I have often slept in the little room and we have never heard anything. There are sundry odd knockings in the house but this could be the old wood expanding or something like that.

For more than 30 years, Betty has been ill with Parkinson's disease. She sleeps in the large front bedroom and has a little bell to ring when she wants attention during the night. Several times she has said, 'Thank you for coming in during the night although I didn't ring my bell' when my wife has been nowhere near the room. A number of times, right up until the late 1980s, Betty has seen the lavender lady walk from the bottom of her bed and disappear through a wall.

INKBERROW

Everyone has heard of Inkberrow, even folk as far afield as Australia and New Zealand, because of its association with 'The Archers'. The Bull, that convivial centre of activity for the everyday folk of the BBC's long-running programme, is based on the Old Bull in Inkberrow which faces the little village green.

Inkberrow had another moment of fame in 1644, during the Civil War, when Charles I chose to sleep at the Old Vicarage. He left his maps there which are still waiting for his ghost to reclaim them; they have now been passed to the county archives for safe keeping.

The Bull's Head

There are two 'Bulls' in Inkberrow: the Old Bull and the Bull's Head which lies on the main road through the village and has more of a local flavour. Most of this building dates back to the sixteenth century. It provides the perfect setting for a ghost - a rabbit warren of rooms with heavy black timbers and low ceilings. The present licensee, Debbie Ison, relates:

> I have never actually seen the ghost, I can only tell you about the little things that have happened which, when put together, suggest there is a ghost here. But I know that at least four people have seen the ghost including two of our guests.
>
> In February 1991 we had a guest staying here and he came downstairs in the morning saying, 'Is my room haunted?' He said that he got out of bed early in the morning and went to the bathroom but just happened to look over his shoulder and saw someone else getting out of his bed.
>
> Another guest said 'I didn't believe you when you said this room was haunted but I woke up and saw a woman sitting on my bed, then she vanished'. He described her as having a long pale-coloured dress.
>
> A few days after we first moved in the regulars began asking if anything had happened yet. Then someone actually said that there was a ghost here. We took it all with a pinch of salt, neither my husband nor I believed in ghosts.
>
> We were told that a woman had been locked in the bedroom over the bar by the ghost and about four or five months after we arrived something strange did happen in that very room. My mother and I were cleaning the bedroom, I went out to get some dusters and as I walked back into the bedroom, the light came on. My mother said, 'Why did it

come on? It couldn't be the ghost, could it?' For a joke, I said 'If there's anybody there, could you switch the light off?' and immediately the light went off. We just put this down to faulty wiring.

We had two dogs at that time and we just couldn't get them into the big room upstairs. One of them was only small and I used to carry him in but as soon as I put him down he would run out again.

Nothing else happened for a short while, then the next incident occurred round about 1969 when Gordon Quiney was here. He often helped us out behind the bar and to save him going home he used to stay the night in one of our single rooms. Each morning he got up very early to let the cleaner in. One morning when I came down, he said 'Where did you get to?' He heard me calling him at about six o'clock, he said, so he got up and went to the door. But no-one was there. Again, a woman's voice called but again, when he went to the door, no-one was there.

On 4 January the following year it was my mother's birthday; she and dad were staying here at the time. We had locked up for the night and everyone in the house was down here, except for my father, Ray. Then my husband went to the door saying 'Ray is calling me'. He went upstairs into Ray's bedroom to see what he wanted and found him fast asleep in bed. Mystified, my husband came downstairs and sat with us, then we all heard a man's voice call again, 'Robert!' My husband went to the stairs and shouted 'Who is it?' but there was no reply. My mother was so frightened she went behind the bar and wouldn't come out.

A few days later something happened that at first I put down to the fact that I was very tired after the Christmas and New Year rush. As I was coming down the staircase I saw the door at the bottom open and a glimpse of a train of a pale-coloured frilly dress - just as if someone had opened the door and pulled the dress through. It was so real that I jumped down the stairs in a couple of seconds and shouted 'Gotcha!' But there was no-one there.

The next incident was really strange. This Yorkshire couple were staying for the weekend and on Sunday morning, the husband came down alone and asked for a beer. As I felt I should stay around in case he wanted anything else, I made myself a cup of coffee and we both sat in the bar, sipping our drinks. Suddenly, a steady trickle of liquid came down from the ceiling. It was just as if someone was pouring half-a-pint of beer from the beam. The husband said 'You've got a leak'. 'That's strange' I said. 'There's no water above there!' And there isn't, just an empty room. I looked to see how large the pool was - and couldn't find it! 'Where the hell is the puddle?' asked the Yorkshireman. It was quite funny, we looked everywhere, even down our boots! 'Well I might not be sober' he said. 'But you are and you saw it!'

This happened again early in 1991. Water started trickling down in the second bar but there is no water supply above and there was no puddle.

We have a lady who does some cleaning and she says that three times she has seen a shadow flitting past the games room window when she knew the place was empty. I was sitting at the top bar talking to my mother when I saw someone in the lower bar. I knew I had locked up carefully.

A friend of mine, Kaye, booked a room upstairs for her son's birthday party. She came early on Saturday morning to put up some balloons and party decorations. She was standing on the table pressing a drawing pin into the wall when she toppled and would have had a nasty fall but, to her surprise, she felt hands holding her tightly on her hips, steadying her until she regained her balance.

The second story about the Bull's Head comes from Betty Kacorevic who was the landlady for nine years. The following incident occurred one July in the 1960s.

We had an American staying here and early one morning I heard him cry out. I leaped out of bed and went to the top of the stairs and there she was, the ghost, walking up the staircase towards me. She had entered the American's room and then come up to the top storey.

She was absolutely beautiful. Just perfect. She had long blonde hair and a white silky dress and she sort of fluttered up the stairs. I was frightened when I heard the American shout but when I saw her I wasn't afraid at all. She never spoke. She got to the top then just disappeared. I suppose she was about fortyish.

The American wouldn't have it that it was a ghost. He kept asking where the beautiful blonde was. I kept telling him 'There is no blonde'.

I heard her several times while I was living here but I only ever saw her this once. And I don't drink, I'm always sober!

Pam Pearce, who helps out at the Bulls Head, provides the third story. In March 1990 she was doing the ironing when, as she relates,

I felt as if someone was there. I have often had this feeling before and put it down to the fact that we treat the ghost as a joke and creep up on each other. However, this time I turned round and saw a young girl just fading. She was wearing a long pale blue print dress with a train, and she had on her head a hat with a scarf over it. I would think her clothes dated back to the sixteenth or seventeenth century. She had long fair hair and was very young and pretty; about 18 or 20, I would guess, but it was all over so soon. I said 'Hullo' but she quickly faded away.

44

According to local tradition a young seamstress died here in about the seventeenth century and it looks as if she comes back to her place of work from time to time. The day I saw her, the landlady had left her sewing things out and I think this is what prompted our ghost to make a return visit.

Ghostly Gossip

A house in the village is said to be haunted. It stands on Rock Hill and once witnessed a suicide.

About three years ago a young man went to visit his friend who now lives in the house. On the table in the bedroom was the top of a stick of deodorant and he saw it move along the table when no-one was near it.

Later the same day, the two young men put side A of a record on which should have taken about twenty minutes, then they went out of the room for a couple of minutes. When they came back side B was just finishing.

*

The story of the ghost of Jo Mucklow is well-known in Inkberrow. The locals say that if you walk past Salter Street crossroads at night you can see the glow of Jo's pipe and hear the rattling of his chains. Darren Roberts relates the story as told to him by his grandfather, who passed the crossroads on his way home from work each evening. He told Darren that he often saw the ghost and just called out 'Evening Joe!'

> Joseph Mucklow was a down-and-out who had lodgings in Little Inkberrow. He fell in love with a beautiful young girl who lived in Salter Street; all day and well into the night he would stand on the corner, puffing his pipe and waiting for a glimpse of her. One day, to everyone's amazement, she agreed to marry him but on the day of the wedding she went to him and told him that he was an ugly, dirty old man and she did not want to have anything more to do with him. He hung himself with a set of chains from a beam in a cart hovel at Morton-under-Hill; and was buried at Salter Street crossroads.

At that time, suicides could not be buried in the churchyard and were usually interred instead at cross roads or T junctions.

Records show that a Joseph Mucklow lived in Inkberrow during the eighteenth century and under the old Poor Law he occasionally received money and clothing. The parish register for 8 November 1773 reads: 'Pauper Joseph Mucklow. Hang'd himself. Buried in Salter Street Crossroad'.

THE PORTWAY AND LILY GREEN

Old Published Reports

The Portway

The Portway is four miles north-east of Redditch as the crow flies, but in the late nineteenth century the journey round country roads, curving this way and that to avoid the hills, would have been well over five miles.

Molly Moor's ghost, according to a communication from Mr. Cocking, of Walford Street, haunted a cottage on the Portway about five miles from Redditch. This was inhabited by a labouring man and wood dealer, of the name of Hunt, who one day related to his three fellow-labourers, Bishop, Carr, and Edwards. some of the extraordinary sights he had seen in his house, particularly mentioning this Molly Moor's spirit, or rather ghost.

His companions were sceptical, and determined to ascertain for themselves whether there was any truth in these statements; and it was agreed that they should go to Hunt's cottage and stay the night for that purpose.

Accordingly ... they took with them a big bottle of ale, and inspired by this in all probability, Edwards protested that if Molly Moor should appear, he would give the ghost a kiss.

At the proper hour, viz., 24 o'clock ... footsteps were heard overhead, and then on the stairs.

"Now for Molly Moor," said Edwards, jumping up to meet the apparition at the foot of the staircase. Then seeing before him the figure of a woman (better looking perhaps than the general run of ghosts) he sprang towards her to keep his word. An awful crash, not of thunder but of crockeryware, glass, and table legs, followed, proclaiming either that the ghost was indignant at such familiarity, or that Edwards in his haste to kiss Molly Moor had fallen foul of something frailer than woman. The three men were afterwards found lying unconscious upon the floor amid a general wreck of household wares and goods, and they assured the person who kindly furnished the statement that they would not go through such another night for any amount of money.

Who this Molly Moor was I have not been able to learn, but amongst six or eight men, women or boys hanged at Washwood Heath for coining*, some three-quarters of a century ago, there was, I am told, one from the neighbourhood of the Portway, and of the name of Moor.

J M Woodward

---

* *'Coining' was the making of conterfeit coins.*

47

Lily Green Farm

Lily Green has, sadly, now completely disappeared. It was situated one-and-half miles north of Beoley and about half a mile to the east of Icknield Street in the direction of The Portway.

The Lily Green ghost was more obstinate (than the Beoley one) and it took a convocation of six, or sixteen (for accounts differ), of the clergy to lay him in the pond near the house. There he lay quiet enough until the pond was mudded, when the ghost got shovelled out in the mud. Being thus set free from his damp dungeon, he recommenced his former labours, and Abraham Baylis, of Headless Cross, assured Mr Fineter ... that he had frequently heard the "old chap" as if he was making a coffin, or coffer, or something of the kind. This was in an upper room of the house, but if anyone ascended the stairs, the sounds ceased and the ghostly workman was not to be seen.

More than one supernatural being seems to have haunted Lily Green Farm. There was a gate near the house through which neither horses nor cattle would go without being driven, and when they were passing through they quivered in every limb and were all in a foam. A former tenant (a Mr Whitmore), going towards the dresser, was startled to see a hand and a ruffled sleeve extend itself from the wall, but whether in welcome or defiance is not stated.

(These tales of the Portway and Lily Green farm were taken from The William Avery Memorial Volumes*)*

REDDITCH

Though much of Redditch is very modern, as a result of its designation as a New Town in 1964, its history stretches a very long way back. The Ridgeway and most of the busy Evesham Road which runs into Redditch were once a prehistoric track along which roamed nomadic man and herds of wild cattle.

Some 3,000 years ago the Celts could have been living in the area, perhaps the large mound of earth near Beoley church was a Celtic hill fort.

Redditch lies in a valley almost entirely surrounded by hills and so it is not surprising that until the twelfth century the centre of Redditch was mostly an inhospitable swamp. A small settlement (known as 'Osmerley') did manage to survive but the history of Redditch really begins when twelve monks arrived in about 1140 to start work on Bordesley Abbey. Workers such as stonemasons, labourers and ironworkers brought their families and settled outside the abbey walls. A ditch runs through the abbey meadows from which the town probably gets its name since the water sometimes runs red from iron oxide (a red ditch). Bordesley Abbey was at its height in the thirteenth century, when it owned land in Worcestershire, Warwickshire and Gloucestershire including twenty granges such as Hewell Grange.

Redditch was fortunate in the aristocratic families who settled locally in the sixteenth century and onwards. The Sheldons and the Windsors, for example, both took an active interest in the welfare of the town. It was partly through the generosity of the Windsors that St Stephen's chapel was transferred in 1805 from the Bordesley site to what had become the centre of the town, a mile away to the south-west.

For the last two centuries or so, the town has been famous for its fishing hooks, springs and needles. The golden eye needles of Redditch were reputed to be the best in the world.

When Redditch became a New Town in the 1960s many of the locals complained about the influx of new residents, quite forgetting that their own great - or great-great-grandparents were probably also newcomers. During the nineteenth century the population increased from 1,000 to over 13,000; so in a sense Redditch has been a new town more than once!

Now. because of the wisdom and aesthetic sensitivity of the old Redditch Development Corporation, we have one of the most successful New Towns in the country. They began work in 1964 and over the next twenty years the population was to increase from 30,000 to 70,000. Their errors of judgement were few, but perhaps one of them was to site the Kingfisher Shopping Centre over an old burial ground......

The Kingfisher Centre

(Introduction by John Lewis, Vice-Chairman of the Bordesley Society)

The paranormal incidents at the Kingfisher Centre, which are described in the newspaper cuttings shown on the following pages, could well be connected with the exhumations which took place when the Congregational Chapel in Evesham Street (the main shopping thoroughfare in 'old' Redditch) was demolished in preparation for the second phase of the new shopping centre. The graves of a large number of Redditch folk in the grounds of this old chapel were then filled in, and the whole area levelled off. The business premises mentioned later are in the vicinity of the site of the chapel.

I was a member of the Special Constabulary at the time, and patrolled the area (on foot) each weekend, between 10 pm and 2 am. A tall 'peep-proof' fence was erected around the chapel grounds while the demolition and exhumations were carried out, and although not of a nervous disposition I vividly recall a feeling of uneasiness, especially when the wind whistled through the chapel and the other partially demolished buildings in this once very well-known Redditch Street.

The once crowded pubs - *The Hungry Man, The Talbot and The Fleece*; and the shops - *Hollingtons, Tom Smith's and Clem Jackson's* - looked extremely sad in the moonlight. If only they had been able to speak!

Hair-raising 🐦

Centre's ghostly secrets

HAIR-RAISING claims that Redditch's prestigious shopping centre is haunted have been backed by several of the night guards.

Guards have complained of an eerie presence in both Cannon Newton House and Kingfisher House and locked doors being mysteriously opened.

Kevin Phillips, Maintenance Manager at the Shopping Centre has said lifts into Cannon Newton House have had to be closed at night because cleaners and guards were getting stuck between floors and had to be released.

He said: "There was no electrical or mechanical reason for it to break down, it is used thousands of times a day, but we had to close the lift because it was happening with such alarming regularity and the lift engineers had no explanation for it."

It has been confirmed by a council spokesman that Mothercare and a toilet block were built on the site of a graveyard and the former congregational Church in Evesham Street.

The bodies were exhumed in 1979 and moved to new burial places but many of the guards believe some were left behind and it is their tortured spirits which roam the centre.

Mr Phillips said: "The most common sighting seems to be a hooded monk in Cannon Newton House who walks out of the pump room and down the corridor.

Dean Mobley, senior night security guard said: "Last week I was on duty with another guard at Evesham Square when he glanced up and went white. He said, can you see that old woman' I glanced up and saw something step behind the pillar and fade away."

A cleaner, who asked not to be named, said: "One night a security guard came to her as white as a sheet saying he had seen a figure in Cannon Newton House. He left the job a few days later.

Evangalist minister Reverend Eric Mullholland said: "I believe in the supernatural, but I do not believe that moving the bodies can have caused this disruption.

"The body decays and fades, it is no longer there, the spirit goes to glory or eternal damnation.

"A lot of the rumours tend to be superstition but I am prepared to go around with the security guards at night to witness this for myself."

John Kelleher, assistant manager at the Kingfisher Shopping Centre said "We would love to find this ghost he owes a fortune in rent arrears.

"But really we are not reall worried about the claims and do not think it affects trade at all."

Redditch Advertiser, 22 February 1989

51

Centre ghost hunt!

THE Redditch Advertiser has been on a ghost hunt — to see if the Kingfisher Shopping Centre is haunted.

An Advertiser reporter and photographer were joined by local medium Ann Jones in the early hours of Saturday morning in Cannon Newton House in a bid to find out what is going on.

Ann believes there are three kinds of ghost sightings.

One she describes as something like a video re-run. An emotional outpouring in the past leaves marks on the atomosphere.

The second type of spirit is one that passes readily between this world and the next and does not mean any harm.

The third are people who died in a violent or sudden way and have lost their way. They may need help to get over to the 'other side'.

Ann began her investigation in Cannon Newton House and walked the path the monk is reputed to walk — but she felt nothing. She believes the monk may well just be what she describes as a video re-run.

Ann reached the corner of the corridor and set off down the other side. She immediately felt colder. She said: "I can usually tell when there is a spirit. The cold is very clammy and different from a draught. I am certain there is a spirit here.

"I feel the pesence of a lady. She is between 30 and 35, 5ft 5in tall. I get the feeling she is lost."

Ann said she felt another presence in the building and asked if any of the workers had been killed in the construction of the shopping centre.

Ann went back to the cold spot again and said: "It feels like a doorway with cold on either side."

She went to the fountain area and felt the same cold spots which matched exactly the cold area above. She said: "I feel we are being watched from above."

Ann said there are areas in the centre she does not like — particularly car part two which she avoids.

She added: "I don't think the old town should have been destroyed. It seems to have stirred up many problems. A new centre was needed but it could have been built further out."

Ann feels there is something strange in Cannon Newton House — perhaps a spirit needing her help. She has asked to visit the centre again at night.

Further investigations have shown a worker died in the Centre.

Ian Mackay of the New Town Commission said: "A worker died in the Kingfisher Centre during its construction.

"I think he fell from scaffolding when car park two was being constructed."

Car park two has seen a man jump to his death from the top and a murder.

Redditch Advertiser, 1 March 1989

Ghostly goings-on at charity sleep-in

GHOSTBUSTING fund-raisers, who spent the night in the "haunted" Kingfisher Centre, claim they came face to face with spooks.

Pat Pascoe, manager of Sharpes Bedrooms who organised the sleep-ins at her store was delighted with the £3,000 raised but was concerned over some of the people's experiences.

She said: "We were raising money for a good cause so you would think the spooks would have left us in peace. But seriously some of the girls who came along did have strange experiences."

Mandy Spooner, aged 18, who was sponsored by friends and colleagues at Dairy Crest to do the sleep-in, wrote after going into the corridor behind the shop: "It is underground. I felt the floor open up and felt myself going down but not coming back up".

Since then Mandy has felt uneasy but has no lasting after effects from her experience.

Pat said: "We invited a medium along — Tom Smith — who went to the same spot the night before the girls and felt a presence.

"Later that evening a security guard came to the door and asked if anyone had gone out of the shop because they heard a shout.

"A few of us rushed to the balcony and one girl said 'can't you see the lady standing beside the door. No-one else could see anything.

"I am now more convinced there is something in the centre and it is perhaps time it was laid to rest."

Pat was warned by two mediums not to go ahead with the sleep-in. Ann Jones, the medium who investigated the centre with the Advertiser, wanted it stopped.

She said: "People do not know what they are dealing with and it can be dangerous to interfere with things.

"I think they were mocking the spirits and should be more careful with what they do not really understand."

Redditch Advertiser, 22 March 1989

Spooks in store

GHOSTLY goings on are causing chaos at a Redditch china shop.

Tills ring, crockery crashes to the floor and paperwork goes missing say staff at Pottery Plus, Kingfisher Centre.

And they have given their 'resident ghost' a name to make him feel more at home.

"We call him Fred', said assistant manager Val Edwards. "I had an open mind about ghosts before I started work here, but there can be no other explanation for the things that happen".

She added: "One morning a stack of leaflets had been arranged in a fan on the floor and soon after some tablemats was laid out the same way.

"I was serving a customer in the basement and a metal shelf support flew across the room and some of the china broke.

"But we have never felt scared. We have just got used to things happening without explanation, like the till ringing when there is no one around".

Redditch Advertiser, 16 May 1991

Quite apart from the newspaper articles, other rumours of ghosts in the Kingfisher Centre are circulating.

A Redditch postman tells the story of a great friend of his who used to be a security guard in the Centre. About six months after the Centre first opened the guard was walking along the balcony by Owen Owen's just after midnight when he felt something behind him. He turned round and there, in the half-darkness, coming straight at him, was a white misty form. Although the details were indistinct he could see that it was the ghost of a tall slim man. The guard was so terrified that he froze, unable to move. The apparition continued gliding quite rapidly towards him, then passed through him and continued its journey. The guard felt an unearthly chill as it passed through his body.

Bordesley Abbey

(Introduction by John Lewis, Vice Chairman of the Bordesley Society, Redditch).

I became fascinated by the rectangular mounds and hollows in the Abbey Meadows as far back as 1935, when I accompanied my parents to the area on a Sunday afternoon walk. I pestered my relatives with questions about them, and I grew up fascinated by the story of the twelve white-robed monks, who arrived over 800 years ago to start building an abbey on this unpromising marshy ground. I learned about their way of life, dedicated to hard work and prayer; how they rose at two o'clock every morning to pray and ate only one meal a day. I discovered that the Cistercian monks were expert artesian engineers, and that they built this impressive abbey, complete with fishponds and a millpond, serviced by a piped water supply, and a proper drainage system. The abbey and the surrounding community flourished because of their hard work and careful husbandry, and from generous donations.

I was told that a small stream with banks of rich red clay, a red-ditch, touched the outskirts of the abbey, and a small settlement developed there, perhaps a group of stonemasons, and the area became known as Redditch. If there had been no Bordesley Abbey, there would be no Redditch.

Later, I used to cycle there on my own, 'armed' with my sheath knife, with which I used to carefully cut through the top layer of grass and soil of the mounds, because even as a schoolboy I was sure that I would find exciting things just beneath the surface - maybe even buried treasure! I did not know that I was investigating what was to become one of the most important medieval sites in Europe.

I didn't find buried treasure, but I did find pieces of tile - some of which had coloured patterns on them, and other pieces, which had a hole in them, which my history teacher at St Luke's School, Rectory Road, Headless Cross, said were roof and floor tiles.

I returned to the meadows on many occasions in the '30s, and because of the river and damp conditions, they were often shrouded in a ghost-like mist which was somewhat unnerving - even uninviting, especially when I learned that over 2,000 skeletons lie in one small area alone, which used to be the churchyard of St Stephen's chapel!

Around that period, I learned about the Sheldons, whose tombs were in the fifteenth century church of St Leonard, which stood like a solitary sentinel on a neighbouring hill. Were the Sheldons (who must have known these meadows intimately) offended at what I was doing? I always felt uneasy, and often glanced nervously in the direction of the church.

When I returned to the meadows thirty years later to carry out exploratory 'digs' with my friends Dorothy Manson and Tom Maries of the Bordesley Society there was still that feeling of mystery, sadness and loneliness that we were all aware of, as we tried to concentrate on our investigations. What tragic events had occurred there, centuries previously? Were we being watched, and were we doing things that we had no right to be doing? We all had this conviction that we were definitely not alone!

Close Encounters

Ben Cooper was well-known in Redditch during the 1960s for his work with young people interested in sport. He was also on the committee of the Bordesley Society. His widow says that her husband was always absolutely certain that he had seen the ghost of a monk near Bordesley Abbey. She says:

When he was about thirteen, he and two or three friends were in the Abbey meadows when they saw this monk in a robe and cowl (a brown habit) gliding slowly towards them. Nothing would shake his story and he was a very down-to-earth man. He told me exactly where it was.

Go past the crematorium gates and on the right-hand side is just a narrow country lane - well he was there and the monk was just at the churchyard by the fir trees, coming across the field onto the stile.

Ann Jones of Astwood Bank says that a number of people have told her about seeing a ghost of a monk in the Bordesley area - on the meadows, walking across the new golf course and even passing through neighbouring houses. She comments:

The figure has always been described as wearing a brown habit which is curious because the monks of Bordesley Abbey were Cistercians and therefore would have been clothed in white. If, however, a monk committed some misdeed he was banished from the monastery and made to wear a brown robe; the suggestion has been made that this is a lost, disgraced monk trying to gain readmittance to Bordesley Abbey.

Old Published Reports

Perhaps the most famous Redditch ghost is the 'Black Hound of Arden', the Earl of Warwick, who was buried in Bordesley Abbey. His nickname was given to him by Piers Gaveston, an insolent, evil young man who was the favourite of the future King Edward II. The Earl of Warwick prophesied that one day Gaveston would 'feel the teeth of the black hound'.

Gaveston made himself so unpopular that he was eventually captured by the local nobility, tried at Warwick Castle and was beheaded at Blacklow Hill, near Warwick in 1312. The Earl of Warwick died in agony from poison administered by one of Gaveston's admirers.

'The black hound' was reputed to haunt the abbey site and he apparently appeared to James Woodward who first excavated there in the 1860's. Mr Woodward describes the incident in wonderful purple prose in *The History of Bordesley Abbey* which is quoted below:

As these tiles* were by no means firmly embedded, it was deemed advisable to set watch over them during the night. For many reasons, natural and supernatural, this was a far from enviable duty, but it was undertaken by the men engaged in the excavations.

One night, however, it befel that no-one could conveniently take the second watch of the night, to wit, from nine to midnight, but myself.

It was a dark and cloudy night, and the wind blew in gusts across the Abbey Meadow, bending the tall poplars by The Forge to and fro, and then dying away mournfully among the pines on Beoley Hill. Though wrapped in many garments it was too cold to remain on the mounds, so retiring to the little Chapel, and sitting down by the base of the square pier, I, like Sir Hudibras,

> *Cheered up myself with ends of verse,*
> *And sayings of Philosophers.*

This, however, failed at last to banish graver thoughts, and the story of the Black Dog of Arden, the grim Earl of Warwick, whose bones perchance they were that had been so lately disturbed, came again and again to the mind - his treachery, his vengeance, his murder and his burial at Bordesley Abbey. St Stephen's clock, striking the hour of midnight, intensified rather than disturbed my train of thought, when a louder blast of wind caused me to raise my head - at that instant another head appeared above the heap of soil on the opposite side of the Chapel - it was the head of a large black dog. It looked at me for a moment, and then disappeared. I seized a crow-bar and climbed to the top of the mound but my visitor was gone.

Unwilling to add to the number of marvellous tales about the Abbey, I said nothing about my sable visitor. But he had already appeared to another, beside myself, in the dead waste and middle of the night, viz., to Twinning, who inquired next morning if I had seen anything extraordinary in the night. Upon pressing him for the reason of his inquiry, he related a story, almost the facsimile of mine, and of the instantaneous appearance and disappearance of what many might have deemed an embodiment of the spirit of the swarthy Earl of Warwick.

Thomas Lowes, the old bellringer of the old chapel there, spoke of a subterranean passage leading towards Beoley or Gorcott Hall, out of which came a night coach driven by the devil or a spectre...

(*From* The William Avery Memorial Volumes)

---

* *The medieval tiles discovered by James Woodward were removed and relaid in the vestry of St Stephen's Church, Redditch. They will eventually be relaid in the new museum on the edge of the Bordesley meadows.*

The Palace Theatre

When the Palace opened in 1910 it was one of the best theatres of its type in England, with an orchestral pit below stage level, a proscenium with an opening 22 feet wide, a stage depth of 22 feet and seating for 700. It accommodated all types of shows - silent films, variety shows, drama, musical comedy, grand and light opera. Redditch was justly proud of its new theatre.

Local drama societies, music societies and operatic groups used the Palace for their public performances; young talent was fostered and several names became well-known, for example, Mavis Bennett, Alan Styler and John Hanson.

However, by 1954 the fortunes of the Palace had declined, partly because of the growing popularity of television, and in May of that year the theatre closed. The following February it opened as a roller skating rink but the stage had been drastically altered and the raked floor had gone. In 1959 the Palace became a dance hall and in the 1960s, a Bingo Hall.

The fate of the Palace hung in the balance as development began on Redditch New Town. Was it going to be demolished and replaced by a shopping precinct? With some relief, the locals heard that it was to remain as a multipurpose theatre, with stackable seats to allow the floor area to be used in a variety of ways. The history of the Palace Theatre continues - but now includes a ghost.

Arthur Bunegar, Technical Manager of the Palace Theatre, has seen the theatre ghost three times: about ten years ago during a rehearsal, in 1988 in the flies and the following year in Box A. He describes his experiences below:

> The Palace is a weird place to be in at night. I have heard chains rattling and moans, and a friend and I once heard a terrible, high-pitched scream.
>
> I last saw the ghost in 1989. We had an assistant stagehand who used to slope off with his girlfriend for a bit of snogging when the circle was empty. This one night I couldn't see him and I thought I would try to find him. I went over the gallery and looked in the circle but he wasn't there. Just as you go through the double doors in the circle there is a door into box A and as I opened this door I felt someone on the other side, whipping the door out of my hand. I felt a rush of cold air and I saw our ghost, Wilfred, standing there. Having the door wrenched out of my

grasp like that really frightened me.

I call him Wilfred for want of any other name. What his real name was I do not know. The story goes that he was an old caretaker who kept a little terrier dog for company. Eventually he lost his dog and he died without finding him. It is said that he still wanders about looking for him.

He's a small man in Victorian dress: high collar, bowler hat, a black cut-away waistcoat and a pin-striped suit. What I particularly remember is a big walrus moustache and round face. I can't swear to it - you only see him for a second, then he's gone - but I believe he has a gold watch chain.

I first saw him when there was a whole crowd of us on the stage. A colleague of mine, Bob Taylor, suddenly noticed a curtain at the back of the auditorium being pulled to one side and he called out 'Can I help you?'. I looked to see who he was talking to and saw this figure standing at the back of the auditorium. Then all of a sudden it just disappeared. About seven years later I caught another glimpse of him, this time in the flies at two o'clock in the morning.

Other people have seen the ghost, too. A year or two back, we were working late near the band room - this is the old part of the theatre (you only ever see him in the old part) when a lad, Steve, went into the band room and came running out as white as a sheet. One of the managers asked him what was the matter and he said he had just seen a ghost. No way could you get him to go back into that band room again!

Then, on the last night of the gang show, we had a party and I noticed a young girl guide sitting in the front row of the circle with her boyfriend. Later, the girl's mother came up to me and said, 'For God's sake don't mention the theatre ghost to my daughter. She was sitting in the circle when she looked down into the orchestra pit and saw the keys of the clavernova moving without any music coming out. She was absolutely terrified!'. The power had been switched off and I had locked the auditorium up so that no-one could have got backstage.

People have put things down which have disappeared; then after searching high and low have found them again half-an-hour later - exactly where they were left. Bob Taylor was recently telling me about somebody who left his shorts out, couldn't find them anywhere and an hour later found them just where he had put them.

I'm not afraid of Wilfred, ghosts don't frighten me. I'm of the opinion that the living can do you much more harm than the dead!

The Palace Theatre could not survive without its team of voluntary staff. For ten years, until the end of the 1980s, Bob Taylor was a voluntary member of the stage crew, building scenery, laying out stage sets, stripping them down again and helping wherever necessary - most evenings, sometimes until 2 am! Bob says:

Although I have never actually seen the ghost, so many ghostly incidents have occurred I do think the Palace must be haunted. I'll just give two examples.

I'm a member of Redditch Operatic Society and about five years ago we were performing 'The Merry Widow'. Because of the shortage of dressing rooms my friend and I were sharing a room normally used for a shower. On the Friday, we had our costumes laid out ready, then at the last minute my cuff links disappeared. This was catastrophic. We hunted high and low for them but couldn't find them and in the end my friend lent me his spare pair. When we came offstage after the performance, there were my cuff links lying side by side next to my shoes, looking as if someone had placed them there very carefully. I said to my friend 'Are you messing me about?' but he assured me that he hadn't put them there.

When I worked backstage there was a little room right down in the basement, only two of us had a key. Every time we left we were very careful to turn the light off yet whenever we went back into the room the light was on again.

Other sightings of the Palace Theatre ghost

The Palace Theatre ghost was seen twice during 1991. One evening in April, a member of the staff saw an elderly man in the box office who faded away into thin air.

In June, a young man was on the stage, having his photograph taken by someone in the boxes. The photographer told the young man to look up, he did so but immediately looked terrified. The photographer asked him what the matter was and he replied that the Palace Theatre ghost was standing in the next box. There were several people in the theatre but the young man on the stage was the only person who could see the ghost.

Ghostly Gossip

Smallwood, Marsden Road

During the 1970s a family who lived in Marsden Road heard strange noises in their house. On most nights, doors would bang or footsteps could be heard going up and down the stairs. The head of the household did not believe in ghosts so he laid trip wires; but he never caught anyone and the footsteps continued.

Then one night, a teenage daughter was woken by the sheets

being pulled back and there, sitting on the bed, was a beautiful lady with long, fair hair and a silky white gown. After a few seconds, she faded away.

Not surprisingly, the family decided to move house.

Beoley Road West, St Georges

In the early 1960s a local man was driving home with his girlfriend from an evening out when he thought he saw a headless person sitting on a wall at the bottom of Beoley Road, where there was a row of six old cottages. He thought he must have been mistaken and drove past. Then his girlfriend said 'Did you see that?'.

He turned the car round to take another look but both the headless man and the wall had gone.

Beoley Road and the Do-It-All Site

Councillor Ann Davies recalls two ghost stories which she heard from her grandmother who lived right in the centre of Redditch near the Co-operative store which features in the second story.

A large house belonging to the Terry family once stood across the road from the site now occupied by Do-It-All in the centre of Redditch. A long time ago - I'm speaking of two or three centuries ago, they had a mentally retarded daughter. In those days children who were mentally defective were shut away and she was kept locked in a room; but she was given an old organ which she played all day and as people went past they could hear the music. Then she died and a few years later her family moved away. But the people who moved in after them found they always had to keep one room locked. The room was always cold and no matter how far the heating was turned up, they couldn't get it warm; and many a night they could hear an organ being played in there. Yet there was nothing in the room, it was always kept empty.

At the top of Beoley Road, where the motorcycle shop now stands, was once a Co-operative store. About fifty years ago a strange family lived in attic rooms above the store. They had a son but nobody ever saw him; then he was found hanged in the attic. After this anyone who was working in the shop at night could hear his ghostly footsteps walking to and fro on the floorboards overhead. This continued until about twenty years ago.

Light industry has played an important part in the history of Redditch and it is therefore surprising that only two stories of industrial ghosts survive, one from the heart of Redditch, the other not far from the centre on the edge of Arrow Valley Park.

Premier Springs, Clive Road

Before Mick became a postman in the early 1970s he worked as a storekeeper at Alcocks Fishing Tackle in the old Premier Springs factory at the end of Clive Road. One dark winter's evening, at about five o'clock, he was sitting at his table in the warehouse, sorting out bundles of wire, when the wires began twitching, then moving of their own accord. Finally, as if they were tossed by an invisible hand, they were jumping off the table and so were his papers and his sandwich box. Absolutely terrified, he looked up just in time to see a dark shape disappearing out of the door. Mick grabbed his coat and ran. He says that it frightened the life out of him.

Eccles Factory, Brook Street

Margaret's parents were caretakers during the 1960's at Eccles factory in Brook Street. Her mother told her the following story.

The owner's son was the manager of the factory but he had not been to work for some months before this particular day as he had been ill. My mother used to do a bit of cleaning before the workers arrived, starting with the manager's office. On this morning, as she went towards the room, she heard a noise, which surprised her because she knew she was the only person on the site. She looked into the office and saw the manager sitting there, with his head under his arm. She cried out, dropped her cleaning materials and ran and fetched my father, although of course by the time they arrived back at the office the apparition had gone. The following day the manager died from a brain tumour.

Old Published Reports

The next two interesting anecdotes were written about a hundred years ago.

How did a farmer cure sick cows before the introduction of modern medicines? One method was to consult a white witch.

Among the "white-witches" of Redditch, I have been informed of two rather eminent in their profession. Being men, they ought properly to be termed "white-wizards," but I have no desire to disturb the settled order of things, and will therefor retain the old appellation. One was a John Johnson living in a cottage near to the old Tan House, a man who in addition to "ruling the stars" sold salves and medicines for man and beast. These remedies had to be prepared or used under the proper celestial influences; and it is a tribute to his skill as a medical man that he was in his own day known as "Dr. Johnson."

He ... was consulted by Farmer ..., who wished to know who had bewitched his cows. The doctor told his client to cut off some hairs from the cows' tails and burn them at midnight, and then lay his horsewhip on the back of the next person who came into the house so as "to draw blood upon him," and the cows would give milk again.

The farmer followed the doctor's advice and the first person who came in afterwards chanced to be "Old Rodney," presumably a *black-witch*, who lived in a cottage at Headless Cross, close to the old *Folly Inn.* The farmer administered the lash, the blood flew out *black,* and the cows got all right again.

The other white-witch was John Smith, who lived somewhere in Red Lion Street. His special *forte* was discovering lost or stolen property; and I am informed that he was consulted "by all the neighbourhood" of former days and did not, like the common fortune-tellers, use cards as their oracle, but cast figures, and cross-examined the stars for information.

> They'd search a planet's house to know
> Who'd broke or robb'd a house below.

Mercury, being the god of thieves, was probably the planet interrogated as to stolen property; while the moon would be plied to in case of highway robbery. Some years ago I was shown, at Crabbs Cross, a silver disc, engraved with planetary signs which had been consulted by the grandfather of the present owner on all important occasions.

Back Street, The Ghost of John the Gardener

This ghost's "walk" was not strictly limited to his head quarters, the old Tan-house, but he sometimes visited one or two of the old cottages higher up the Back Hill. Not being able to sleep quietly in his own narrow bed, he so far envied the living as to wake them up from theirs in the dead of night by causing a noise resembling that of a cart-load of gravel being shot upon the roof over their heads. That some such noises did actually take place, I have the word of an ear-witness of undoubted veracity and intelligence, and that of another whose sincerity I could not doubt, but whose mind was inclined to believe in low forms of the supernatural. She had seen the ghost as well as hear him, but he only appeared to her in a brute form, sometimes that of a dog, at other times that of a rabbit, but always white. On one occasion (as she informed me) when her husband, then but a sweetheart, came courting her, they met in the garden, and while they were engaged in conversation a white beast darted between them and they both darted off; the damsel flew into the house and the lover ran off down the hill. That night it seemed as if the roof were being broken in over her head by showers of stones! This event, though it interrupted the course of true love for an evening, did not stop it; for the courtship ended in a marriage now dissolved by death.

(*Both of these anecdotes are from* The William Avery Memorial Volumes)

Batchley

Mr D is a sensible, practical ex-lorry driver, not the type of person normally associated with paranormal experiences. Yet here he is, wondering whether or not he has 'second sight' and with a repertoire of ghost stories at his fingertips.

I could have inherited the gift of second sight from my mother's side. I try to avoid it as it can be very frightening. I sometimes dream about national disasters before they occur, floods, tornadoes and so on, although I can't usually tell which area of the world they're in. The night before the Lockerbie disaster I dreamt that a plane exploded in the air. I hate to think of any harm coming to anybody.

The first memorable experience I had of second sight was when I took my driving test. I just knew that, in a few years' time, I would have to take the test again. A few years later I did lose my licence and had to retake the test.

When I was eighteen I was driving lorries for my dad and I had this strong feeling that I should not take a certain lorry out that day. I told my dad that if I went out I would get stopped and, sure enough, as I was driving through West Bromwich I was called to one side by a Ministry of Transport spot check and my brakes were found to have a fault.

I'm not the sort of person who reads a lot of books or sits watching films. However, when I went to visit Caernarvon Castle I could see through my imagination the people who lived there in the past, I knew how all the rooms were used. I was telling my wife when another woman, who happened to overhear, asked me how I knew all that when I hadn't bought a guide.

I do predict the weather. I'm well-known among my friends for doing this. The lady I work for, for instance, had a choice of two dates for her daughter's wedding and asked my advice. I told her to take the first date because the morning would be fine and although there would be a thunderstorm in the afternoon the weather on the second date would be even worse. She did what I said and was pleased with my recommendation.

I have seen a lot of ghosts. The first ghost - in this case I should call it a vision - that I ever saw was a driverless car (a convertible) travelling up the Lickeys from Barnt Green and then vanishing. I was in a car with three others going in the opposite direction. Three of us saw the ghostly car but not the lad who was driving us.

In the late 1960s I was driving towards the Red Lion Public House in Alvechurch about 7.30 in the evening when an elderly man wandered out into the road in front of me. I braked sharply, then sat in the car and watched him go by. I saw him walk through the rails on the edge of the pavement, then vanish. I went into the pub and there was the man who had just vanished, sitting having a pint. It wasn't until a few months later, when I'd become a regular at the Red Lion, that I learned that the father of the man at the pub had been killed at the spot where I had seen the ghost, and that father and son looked very much alike.

The house that we live in now is haunted. As soon as we moved in my younger son and I both felt that someone else was living there. We can hear strange bumps and bangs upstairs. On three occasions my sheets have been tugged from me in the middle of the night, which frightened me so much that I swore and told them or it to get off. Then during the last twelve months I have twice seen the white form of a woman on the landing at the top of the stairs. I have started to go up the stairs, looked up and seen her. I can't really judge her height from the bottom of the stairs but she's quite slim and seems to wear a white nightdress. Because I can't see her face clearly, I assume that she is wearing a hood and I am looking at her from the rear. She fades away after a few seconds. I'm told that the woman who lived there before us died in the house and the only explanation I can think of is that this is her ghost.

Beoley

People have probably been living at Beoley for more than 3,000 years. Near the entrance to Beoley Church, opposite the war memorial, is a tiny hill which was once the foundations of a hill fort. These fortified homesteads were mostly built between 1,500 and 150 BC so the Beoley hill fort could date from that time, although it

Beoley Vicarage

has not yet been excavated. It was perhaps once inhabited by several generations of Celts, of a very different culture to ours. They believed that spirits inhabited natural phenomena such as trees, springs and rocks.

The ugly heads of Beoley font have been witnessing infant baptisms for over eight hundred years. The church was built in 1140, possibly by a settlement of iron workers as it is dedicated to their patron saint, Saint Leonard. They would have been attracted to the area by the plentiful supply of timber (Beoley was on the edge of the forest of Arden) and the easy access, for Beoley lies on Icknield Street.

The history of Beoley is dominated by the Sheldon family who came to live in the Beoley area when Ralph Sheldon married Joyce Ruden early in the sixteenth century. At one time they were one of the two richest families in England. Their family vault lies beneath the chantry chapel of Beoley Church.

Ralph's great nephew, William, was responsible for much of the good fortunes of the family. He achieved respect and admiration, first from his contemporaries for acquiring great wealth and status, and secondly from posterity for devising the exquisite and priceless Sheldon tapestries. The Sheldons were already a famous weaving family when William sent his son and an employee to Arras, a town famous for its tapestries, to study the art of weaving. By also employing some Flemish weavers, he achieved a high standard of work. But it was a stroke of genius - the idea of creating tapestry maps - that resulted in the beautiful tapestries the family has long been famous for.

Beoley Church and Vicarage

Mrs Grace Judge, who tells the following anecdote, lived at the vicarage from 1955 to 1969, when her husband was the vicar.

> I always felt that Beoley vicarage was haunted. It had an eerie atmosphere. I used to hear all sorts of strange noises - footsteps and other things moving about the house. It was a very eerie atmosphere. All kinds of peculiar things happened. For example there was often a terrible smell, as if a potty had been under the bed for ages! This stench would move from one bedroom to another; but we were sure it was nothing to do with rats or mice or anything. The parishioners said there

was a haunted house in the village which they wouldn't walk past at night, but they wouldn't tell me which house it was. I was sure it was ours.

I always assumed it was haunted by one of the Sheldons. The Sheldon vault is in Beoley church. When I went down into the vault, I found that one of the coffins had disentegrated, and so a surviving Sheldon relative arranged for the body to be 'recoffined'. About a hundred years ago, in order to raise funds, the rector at that time opened the vault to the public; but it must have upset the Sheldons for the hauntings began from then. That rector was so sure that a ghost of one of the Sheldons stood at the bottom of his bed every night and looked at him that he paid a man from the village to sleep in the house.

My husband used to go out on a Friday night to a Men's Club. The front door opened onto a large square stone block with a metal draught excluder along the bottom. As you opened the door you heard this 'squish'. Each Friday night I sat in the lounge sewing or knitting and when I heard the 'squish', I would look up, expecting to see my husband come in. But no-one would appear. So I would go to the door and, to my surprise, find it shut and nobody about.

My husband took no notice of my fears until the day he went down with flu. He was supposed to be opening some sort of fete in the village hall and so the headmaster of the school offered to take his place, as well as collecting me and taking me there. As I left the house I decided to lock the front door. When I returned, my husband said, 'Am I glad to see you back! I have been onto the landing and down into the hall a couple of times - I kept hearing the front door opening but there was no-one there!' I told him that the door had still been locked when I came back. He was more sympathetic, then!

In 1969 we left Beoley vicarage and moved to Hanbury. The day after we moved out, two painters and decorators went to Beoley vicarage to renovate it for the next incumbent. They were local people so I knew both of them; the younger man was one of our bellringers.

I remember, it was hot summer day. They were working in the hall when they heard somebody ask a question. They both looked up and saw the figure of a woman dressed, as they described it, in 'fancy costume'. They were too taken aback to reply, and she quickly vanished. The first thing our bellringer did was to hop onto his motorbike and come over to tell us about it. We thought this must be the ghost that had been troubling us while we were there.

I was very annoyed. I had been there fourteen years, I thought to myself, and she had never once appeared to me. Yet here she was, revealing herself to two workmen who had only been in the house a short time!

Mrs Judge contributes another ghost story which she heard while living in Beoley:

> One of our parishioners used to walk acros the field from Beoley to Bordesley on her way to and from school. One day she saw a figure going in front of her, dressed in a long robe with a hood. He climbed over the stile and she went to follow him but almost instantly he disappeared.

A retired lady who once lived in Beoley tells a strange tale:

> About forty years ago, a lady who came to clean for the vicar looked out of an upstairs window and saw a woman in the garden collecting flowers and putting them in a large basket. She ran down the stairs and out the door but the woman had disappeared.
>
> A few weeks later it happened again. The cleaner rushed out and said to the woman, 'Have you been given permission to collect these flowers?' but the woman disappeared. Later, the cleaner told the vicar what had happened and the vicar asked her describe the lady. She gave an accurate picture of his wife, who had passed away a couple of years previously. One of her hobbies had been flower arranging. Each week, she had gone into the garden and carefully selected a variety of flowers which she had then laid in a large basket over her arm.

Carpenter's Hill

The ghost of a monk, usually in a dark habit, has apparently been wandering round Redditch over the last few decades. It has been seen in the Kingfisher Centre, in the Bordesley meadows, in a house in Salter's Lane and at the Old Rectory (Ipsley). Ann Jones suggests that this is a disgraced monk trying to gain readmittance to Bordesley Abbey. The young lady telling this story gives a further clue to his identity.

> I'm going back to 1987 now when I started meddling around with tarot cards. I'll never mess with them again, I can tell you. I had no trouble before then but afterwards lots of peculiar little things started happening. The lights fused. Plates fell off the wall for absolutely no reason. My hair was pulled upwards as if it were stuck to a piece of wood when I was standing in the middle of a room. Shelves which were quite robust have given way. The most curious part of it all, though, was this feeling I had that something was there. Then last week a friend came to see me and as we were sitting talking together late one evening she saw behind me the dark shape of a monk!

I have been down at the library looking up this area. Nearby was Chapel Farm, and I read that a monk burned it down. It's all overgrown now.

I've also heard many stories of paranormal phenomena in this area. It used to be part of the old Arden Forest and I think a lot of worshipping of Pagan Gods was practised here.

Old Published Reports

The clergy of Beoley seem to have been good hands at laying ghosts. One troublesome spirit of an old priest persisted in carrying on his ghostly duties after death, to the annoyance, presumably, of Parson Gittins, then "the man in possession," who at last succeeded in laying his rival under a big tree at the back of his vicarage.

There is a pit at the top of Cockshut Hill (Beoley), where, many years ago, a charcoal burner was suffocated by the fumes from his fire, and here his ghost manifested its presence by a supernatural crackling amongst the thorns round the pit, causing those who heard it to rush with alarm from the spot.

Near the same spot Mr William Guardner saw his own "death token" a week or so before he fell off a hay rick and died in consequence of the fall. Crossing the fields homewards on a fine summer's evening, he was surprised to see before him a man exactly resembling himself in dress and figure, in short, a "double". The apparition kept before him at the same distance and on coming to the stile leading into the Watery Lane, vanished. Mr Guardner related the occurrence when he reached home and shortly afterwards met with the accident which caused his death.

From the cross roads at the foot of Beoley Hill up to the church gate the Beoley goblin played his pranks upon passengers. His especial delight being to jump up behind a horseman, who was lucky if he got up the hill without a fall, the horse becoming unmanageable as soon as the goblin was on his back. On arriving at his limit, the church gate, the troublesome spirit vanished, laughing in his glee at the distress of both man and beast.

The goblin seems to differ from the demons in being mischievous rather than downright wicked in his intentions, nay, some goblins are capable of doing goood actions, especially such as going on with the work of the industrious man, or maid, when these are resting from their labours during the hours of sleep.

(*From* The William Avery Memorial Volumes)

Near the centre of the village is a farm labourer's cottage. On a number of occasions the present inhabitants have seen a shadow falling upon their living room window as if someone outside were walking past to reach the back door. However, when they open the door, no-one is there. The shadow is thought to be the ghost of a former inhabitant.

*

The ghost of a man with a horse and cart has been sighted several times in Beoley. Until the 1820's the main road from Redditch into Birmingham went through the village to join Icknield Street. The River Arrow which crossed the road was usually a shallow ford; but when heavy rain caused the mills upstream to open their floodgates it could become a sudden and highly dangerous flood. In the 1750's, John Wesley was nearly drowned at the ford; in 1810 five horses from a Birmingham brewery were drowned there; in 1820 a Mr Heath lost his son in the floodwaters; in 1825 Mr Turner's horse freed itself from the gig and perished in a part of the river called 'Hemmings Hole'; and in 1861 Henry Garfield drowned there. Rumour says that the ghost is that of a man who would not leave his horse when it was drowning and so lost his own life. The curious thing, however, is that the records do not show a man and a horse being drowned at the same time.

*

One ghost more easily identified is that of Moses Shrimpton, the itinerant who was hung for the murder of Police Constable James Davies in 1885. This murderous shadow has been seen occasionally making its shuffling and unkempt way around the roads of Beoley.

P C Davies lived and worked in Beoley and was much loved and respected by the community. When he was found one morning with his throat cut the horror of the village reverberated throughout the nation. Thousands of people attended his funeral, among them policeman from all over England who left their horses and coaches at Beoley Village Inn.

The most likely explanation for the murder is that Davies was attempting to arrest Moses for poaching. The itinerant might have been strong but he was not very good at covering up his his tracks:

not only did he leave a trail of footprints but he also gave his lover, Jane Morton, P C Davies' watch to sell. Jane was hung with him.

A stone marks the spot where the policeman was found in Icknield Street not far from Bordesley Garage. The original stone has worn away and a second stands close by, recording simply, JD 1885.

Church Hill

One of the last of the new-town areas to be built, Church Hill was, at the time, the showpiece of the Redditch Development Corporation. A central pool is surrounded by shops and the YMCA complex.

The Roman Icknield Street ran straight through the area from north to south but it has now been reduced to a footpath.

This is one of the ghost stories which Councillor Ann Davies remembers being told by her grandmother.

> Before Church Hill, Matchborough and Winyates were built, there used to be a farm called Bomford's Farm and opposite to the barn where the farmer stored his hay was a large marlpit which had filled with water to form a pool. Each time the pit was emptied, it formed a pool again. There was a rumour that it was the entrance to a tunnel which ran from the marlpool back into the Bordesley Abbey ruins. It was said that it was used by the monks as an escape route when King Henry VIII's troops came to pull down the monastery. From time to time, horses' hooves could be heard galloping down this tunnel; nothing was seen, there was just the sound.
>
> Over the last five years the marlpool has been filled in and two houses have been built on it. In the one house, in particular, strange things have happened, for example, the residents would go to bed at night, locking all the doors and turning off the lights, but in the morning the lights would be on and the front door ajar. Eventually they moved out and I know that the house has been sold three times.

Greenlands, Studley Road

Contributed by a local man who comes from an eminent Redditch family. He has written his own story to ensure that his identity is not revealed in any way.

When you read this story you will see why I have not given my name.

One of my relatives was a well-known businessman with a large family who lived in a house in Studley Road. On entry, the hallway was panelled in oak which gave a distinct smell of coffins. There were several strange occurrences which seemed to have no logical explanation. Sometimes the Alsation dog used to take long sniffs under the living room door which led to the hall, his hair would rise along his spine and he would swiftly run to the window, open it with his muzzle and jump out with the cat following. The house used to have a landing balcony and from time to time something moved along it trying all the doors.

One of the grandchildren was born at the house with deformed legs (back to front). It was also rumoured that a child was born in that property previous to this family with features resembling a calf but it did not live for long.

Once, a child lying in his cot in one of the bedrooms was found by one of the parents being observed by the ghost of an elderly man which moved towards the fireplace and disappeared when the parent spoke.

After several happenings and unexplained experiences the family sold the house.

Ipsley

Ipsley is both a parish and a village. The parish comprises five districts, Greenlands, Woodrow, Matchborough, Winyates and Winyates Green. The village contains three large buildings: a palatial office block; St Peter's Church which is old enough to be mentioned in the Domesday book; and Ipsley Court, the home of the Huband family and, during the eighteenth century, of the poet Walter Savage Landor.

The Old Rectory

The Old Rectory is aptly named, as parts of the building are about a thousand years old! It was probably once the home of the lord of the manor, Sir John Huband, and his ancestors, before he moved to Ipsley Court. The vicars of Ipsley Church were allowed to live there rent free. It has now been converted into a hotel in which early medieval, Elizabethan and nineteenth century architecture has been blended with twentieth century comforts.

The rectory ghost appears in a large room at the front of the house which was once a chapel. A priest's hiding hole runs from here to rooms on two other floors. Tony Moore, the owner, regards his ghost with affection and calls him 'Charlie'.

We first heard about Charlie some twenty years ago when my eldest son, Edward, was four. The three children used to sleep in this room, and one morning Edward said 'Who came into our bedroom during the night? The person came over and looked at me in my bed, then went over to the cot and looked at the baby, and then came over here and looked at Jonathon. Then - he just went!'

We asked Edward to describe him. 'He had a thing on his head', he said, showing us how it came up to a point, 'then it went straight down to the ground'. Isn't that, for a four-year-old, a perfect description of a monk's habit?

The vicar from Bridbrooke (in Warwick) and his wife were once staying here and they said somebody had crossed the room during the night but they hadn't heard the door open, nor the shuffling of feet on the carpet.

A year or two later another couple sleeping in this room asked us 'Is our room haunted?' We hadn't mentioned the subject, so the idea came from them, not from us. It seemed that on the first night the husband had got up during the night, rather surprising his wife because he didn't do that at home. The next night he got out of bed again and walked across the room. This time she sat up in bed and there was her husband fast asleep - he hadn't budged! In retrospect she realised that there had been no noise of footsteps walking over the carpet.

Lodge Park, Salter's Lane

From this very old lane, along which pack horses laden with salt once toiled, comes the next anecdote which is told by a girl in her early teens.

When my step-dad moved into our house in Salter's Lane he felt a strange atmosphere. He said that it was cold and weird. He had only been in the house for two weeks when he woke up just before midnight, choking and gasping for breath. Then he realised that cold hands were pressing on his neck. Shaken and amazed, he opened his eyes to see the tall figure of a monk in an all-black habit leaning over him, gripping him by the neck. My step-dad was looking up into the cowl but there was no face there, just an empty hood. He stretched out for my mom by his side in the bed and tried to wake her; but he couldn't speak and he could only move a little, so couldn't wake her. He was terrified.

He had once been a Catholic but at the age of sixteen had decided not to have anything more to do with religion, but now he remembered his prayers and began saying them. The thing disappeared and my step-dad was able to wake everybody up.

We thought he must have had a bad dream but just two weeks later something else happened which made us wonder if there was something in it. This terrible knocking started. It went all through the kitchen, walls, cupboards and everything. After that a relative of my step-dad's, a Catholic priest, was asked to come and bless the house. He did this, and we heard no more strange noises. As soon as we could, we moved house.

Matchborough

A mother of three teenage children tells a curious story about a ghost which haunted not a building but herself. Was she suffering from epileptic fits as the specialist suggested? If so, why did a cousin experience the same symptoms and why was the ECG normal? Were her experiences the result of deep depression, or was she 'possessed'? She would like to know the answers to these questions as much as anyone.

I should first tell you that I'm a bit psychic. For as long as I can remember I could predict that things were going to happen. I would say to my brother 'Go and answer the door' and he would say 'Why? There's nobody there!'. Then somebody would knock.

I remember one incident at school when I was very young. A new girl, whom I had never seen before, was standing in the cloakroom with three other girls round her and suddenly I knew what she was going to do next. I had experienced this scene before in a dream. I knew that she was going to pull out a silver chain around her neck, open a square silver locket and show everyone a long concertina of tiny pictures. She did just that. They were all religious pictures as her family were very strong Roman Catholics.

I used to be able to tell what people were going to say to me. I lost many friends that way because people don't like you saying something just before they say it. They think you're weird. I split up with my first long-term boyfriend because of this. His mind must have been very easy to read because I knew absolutely everything he was thinking and what he was going to do. This became obvious when we played cards together. I always had the next card ready in my hand before he'd put the last one down. Of course, I always won. It was impossible for us to play cards together. In the end, it got too scary for him and, after two years, we parted.

I saw my first ghost when I was thirteen, although I thought nothing of it at the time. My family went up to Scotland for Hogmanay and we stayed with my grandmother. As I went into the bedroom which had been made ready for me I saw a large hump moving under the bedclothes. I asked my grandmother who was sleeping in my bed. 'No-one', she said but afterwards I heard her telling my mother that it was the bed of my grandfather who had died four years previously.

When I was about fourteen or fifteen I began to be haunted by a personal ghost. I had been living with my grandmother in Scotland but I decided I wanted to return to England to live with my mum and dad. I used to sleep on a massive settee in the front room. One night I was lying in bed, tired yet wide awake, when I heard something breathing strangely, very loud and heavily. I knew something weird was going to happen. Then everything went completely silent, no traffic, no little household noises, nothing. I was scared stiff, absolutely terrified and completely rigid - I could not move any part of my body. A loud, high-pitched humming noise began, boring firstly into each side of my forehead, then into the middle of my forehead with a terrific explosion. I can't describe the pain, it was terrible. But on top of this was the feeling that someone was standing there, watching, just out of sight, someone who didn't want to be seen. If only I could move my eyes and look at him, I would break the spell. But even though the pain went I was still held rigid. I could see, but could not move my eyes. I could feel my hands, but could not move them. And all the time there was this loud breathing as if through a loudspeaker.

After a few minutes, everything eased off and the feeling of terror disappeared. In fact, I felt quite relaxed and relieved.

My personal ghost paid me a visit quite frequently, sometimes as often as once a week for a few weeks, then perhaps with a break of a couple of months. I used to lie in bed, wondering if he would visit me that night. The only time he stopped was when I moved house, then he would disappear for twelve months or so. It was as if he had lost me and had taken all that time to find me again.

When I was twenty I had a bedsitter in Mount Pleasant. My cousin came to stay with me for a holiday, and of course we became quite close. I told her one day about my personal ghost and she told me the same thing had happened to her since she had staying there. She never came for a holiday again.

Sixteen years ago I moved to Matchborough. Nothing happened for about two years, then my ghost found me and paid me visits so frequently that it got me down. I went to see my doctor who sent me to a psychiatrist. He said it sounded like epileptic fits or deep depression. I told him that that was rubbish, I was never at all depressed, that the ghost had come during many of the happiest times of my life and that he always came when I was totally relaxed. However, I had a series of tests and an ECG but nothing showed up, all was normal. I was prescribed tranquillisers and the ghost disappeared for a short time, then came back.

I decided that I was going to have to face the ghost and get rid of him. I knew that if only I could take a look at him, he would go. Each night my husband (who is not at all psychic) slept on his back and I slept on my side, with my hand up my husband's pyjama sleeve, clutching his forearm. The strange thing was that, although I went to sleep like this, after my ghost had been I often found myself about two feet away from husband, with my back to him, squashed against the bedroom wall. I decided that I would also sleep on my back, so that I could see all round the bedroom.

I particularly remember that evening. The sky was that luminous pale blue that we get sometimes in the evening in summer. I lay in bed waiting for something to happen, on my back but with my hand up my husband's sleeve. Suddenly, I felt a gentle, tingling feeling on top of the covers, as if a hundred spiders were running over me, starting at my legs but working all the way up.

Then I heard the whirring noise and felt the boring at my temples. I thought 'I'm going to see who you are!'. I tried to say it out loud but could not manage to form the words. I knew that I must look at him there and then. With a great effort of strength I sat up and knew immediately that I had broken the hold. I had won! I looked about quickly and at the far end of the bed I just caught an impression of someone - a shadow, perhaps a man - when my husband, in his sleep, sat up in bed and blocked my view.

I have never been visited since.

Moons Moat

Moons Moat is now a busy industrial and commercial area and it comes as some surprise to find it described in all the old records as 'a weird and lonely place', so dreadful that when 'great winds swept down the Arrow vale they paused as if affrighted'!*

Ghosts and spirits lurked in this 'ghoul haunted woodland'. Lady Moon (or Mohun) is said to walk on the eve of St Agnes (January 21st). The Moon family lived in a moated grange here but had died out by the middle of the eighteenth century. Mariolle Moon was murdered by Captain Hill in 1693 (see Alcester section, The Angel Inn) adding to Moons Moat's macabre past.

---

* *Information and quotations from* The Story of the Angel Inn, Alcester *by Aubrey Gwinnett.*

Another ghost is reported in *The William Avery Memorial Volumes.*

> Between Beoley and Ipsley lies that lonely spot called Lord Moons Moat, "Moon" being probably a contraction of "Mohun". The ghost, however, haunting this spot is by no means an aristocratic one, being merely a voice crying in the wilderness,
>
> > "Milk and water sold I ever,
> > Weight and measure sold I never."
>
> The loneliness of the spot ought to have furnished us with something more romantic than the ghost of a wretched adulteration of food and giver of short weight and measure. It is, perhaps, owing to the Adulterations Act, and the vigilance of the police that this kind of ghost is now extinct.

Webheath, Birchfield Road

A sixteen-year-old girl had such a macabre experience ten years ago that she can remember every detail as if it happened only yesterday.

The episode began pleasantly enough when her aunt bought her a quaint doll from an antique shop for her birthday, about ten inches tall with brown hair, a white frilled blouse and a patterned skirt. Proudly she displayed it on the desk in her bedroom; but a few days later a strange incident occurred:

> I went to bed at night just as normal, but in the middle of the night I woke up with the feeling that something had disturbed me. My night-light was on and I could see that there was nothing unusual. I noticed my doll sitting on the desk the other side of the room just where I had left it. I looked away for a moment then something caught my eye and I looked back. The doll was standing. Then she started walking along the top of the desk, turned round and walked back again. Backwards and forwards she went. I was really scared and hid under my blankets. I peeped out a few minutes later and she had gone. I thought she was probably on the floor but I wasn't going to stay and find out. I ran next door to my brother's room and shut both doors so that the doll couldn't come in. I spent the night in there, and I had to put up with a lot of teasing from my brother over the next few days. Everybody said I had had a bad dream, but I made sure that the doll was put in another bedroom.
>
> About three months later we went on holiday and a family with three young boys came to look after the house for us. They weren't people that we knew, so we didn't tell them about the doll. Afterwards

we heard that the two boys who slept in the room where the doll was kept had been complaining that it kept moving about during the night. When he heard this my dad threw the doll on the bonfire.

Winyates

Winyates lies to the east of Redditch and was developed during the 1970s as part of the new town. The area was originally part of the Ipsley marshes where 'bob-a-lanterns' or 'will-o-the wisps' could be seen flitting about on a warm humid night. The name comes from Winyates farm which has now been converted into a craft centre.

Ghosts are usually associated with old buildings but this is not always the case and Tillington Close provides an example of a haunted house which is only twenty years old. The woman who tells this story is married with a grown-up family and most of her children have now left home.

My husband and I have seen the ghost at least ten times. It's mostly in the kitchen that she appears, behind the dividing bar. I was standing at the kitchen sink one day only last week when I saw her there. Sometimes I see the ghost when I'm alone, occasionally my husband sees her and sometimes we both see her at the same time.

She wears a flimsy white dress with a shawl draped halfway across her face. She's only there for a second or two - as soon as you see her, she's gone - so I've never actually seen her face. She's tall and her hair is greyish.

My daughter has experienced her, too, although she has never seen her. She has felt her breathing down her neck. One day she went into her bedroom and as she opened the door all the brushes flew off her dressing table.

Our ghost is very mischievous. We never know what we're going to find next. My husband bought a new pair of shoes and as he wanted to keep them in good condition he put stretchers in. I had some new sandals with no backs in which I put on the other side of the hall. When we came down in the morning the stretchers had been taken out of my husband's shoes and put in my sandals!

The day before yesterday I opened a carton of milk and wedged it firmly inside the fridge. Later, when I opened the fridge door, the carton of milk was lying on its side and milk was pouring out. There's no way it could have fallen over naturally.

One evening, my daughter and I were sitting with the windows and door closed and a piece of paper shot up into the air, floated round the room all at the same level, then fell to the floor. I picked it up and placed it in a really thick book. We both went out of the room and when I returned the paper was on the floor again.

One night, when I had gone to bed, my husband went to the outside loo. I could hear all this banging and my husband shouting, 'Cut it out, will you?'. He thought it was me, but I was in bed almost dying with laughter. It was our ghost, banging on the loo door. She banged so hard the toilet roll holder the other side nearly fell off.

There are some flats nearby and we think she once lived there. The neighbours tell us that when the flats were first built a girl named Tracey from the flats often came to this house. She had a lot of problems and eventually committed suicide.

Ghostly Gossip

In Winyates stands a block of six terraced houses which is haunted by the ghost of an elderly man. Almost every year he is seen by one or other of the tenants but he more often makes his presence known by moving things around. A saucepan can go missing in one house only to turn up two houses down the block!

Woodrow

Considering that Woodrow is part of the new town it has a surprising amount of paranormal activity. Many of the residents have snippets of ghostly gossip to tell. A horse and carriage has been seen driving through Woodrow at night more than once; a man in gaiters and old-fashioned clothing walks though the centre; shadows of people fall on the windows of an entire block of flats when there is no-one outside; and at a house in Astley Close ghostly voices and conversations are heard.

Some residents wonder if Woodrow has been built on a 'ley line', a subtle line of earth energy, some argue, which produces a high energy flow and results in increased paranormal activity. The existence of ley lines is as controversial as the existence of ghosts. In 1925 Alfred Watkins noticed that many ancient sites were in alignment, but it was not until 1970 (thirty-five years after Watkins' death) that any great interest was shown in his work.

Woodrow residents have sometimes pointed out that the Ley's High School stands at the area's south-east edge; but the word 'ley' comes from the old English word for a clearing or natural space in a forest area and in this instance is unlikely to have any connection with ley lines.

Rushock Close

A ghost story told by a man who is sceptical about the paranormal is always of particular interest, chiefly because of its probable authenticity.

About five years ago new neighbours moved in next door. They were a young couple and were always popping round to ask this and that. We tried to help them as much as we could and we were very friendly with them.

Then about eight months after they had moved in the girl came round and was clearly petrified. She looked - well, as if she had seen a ghost. Fear, excitement and shock are three words that describe the state she was in, although she was always in control of what she was saying. As she walked into the hallway all the lights flickered and went off, then came on again.

Her husband was away at the time and so she had come to us for help. We calmed her down and she told us what had happened. Furniture had moved, ornaments had crashed and she had seen things float across the room. Apparently, there had been a build up of these instances over the previous month. She had first noticed little things, like putting something down, only to find it disappeared and turned up somewhere else. Then she had noticed things moving of their own accord. But finally on that night it got to the stage where objects were being smashed against a wall.

She couldn't bear the thought of going back into the house after that; so she went to live with her mother in Herefordshire and they sold up and moved away from the area. When her husband cleared out the loft he found a Ouji board, books on witchcraft and all kinds of things to do with black magic. A single woman lived in the house before them and she must have been meddling around with magic.

They had the house exorcised by a vicar and a couple of other people. The vicar came round to our house afterwards just to check that everything was fine.

I tend to be sceptical about these things. But it was more than coincidence the way the lights flickered and went out; and something terrible must have happened judging from the state she was in.

Poltergeists and ghosts are not supposed to haunt the same building at similar times, but they do in the following story. As the haunting is an unpleasant one, no information has been given which could possibly identify the house. The narrator comes from neighbouring Matchborough.

About seven or eight years ago I had a friend who lived with his family in Woodrow. We have, unfortunately, lost touch with each other over the years. He was about fifteen or sixteen at that time and he lived in a block of five houses, all of which had manifestations of one kind or another; but no other house suffered as much as his. Something happened nearly every night or every day - it didn't seem to make much difference whether it was night or day.

The family would go into the kitchen and see a cloud of steam, as if the kettle had been boiling-but the kettle would be cold. The cloud would remain there for half an hour or so before it faded away. There would be sentences written on the kitchen windows, as if someone had breathed on the windows then written with a finger-but the writing would remain for some days. They tried to read the sentences but they were all 'Yea's' and 'Thee's' and the family couldn't make out the meaning.

Articles would move across the table. Items would disappear from one room and reappear in another. The lights would go on and off inexplicably and electrical appliances would be switched on and off. They were woken up several times in the early hours of the morning, for example, by the kettle boiling away. They were also awoken at night by peculiar noises and strange smells. The smells were either the perfume of a flower or the not-so-pleasant odour of a farmyard. Nor would animals willingly enter the house. Any cat or dog carried indoors would shoot outside again.

My friend did not seem to be very worried by all this. He told me that the manifestation never did any personal injury to him. Apart from one time, when his mother burnt her hand on a kettle which had mysteriously been switched on, the family were not hurt physically in any way.

Three or four times, when his mother was walking from the bathroom to the living room, she saw a woman, wearing a long black skirt, dark tight-fitting bodice and a white cap, in the process of being hung, with legs kicking and so on. This 'vision' had no colour in it, it looked as if it were on black-and-white television.

My friend's mother was not the only person to witness this: a number of people saw it, including a priest. But the last time she saw the vision she got fed up and decided to make a fuss. She had the police in, surveyors, social services and the borough council. Finally, the house was exorcised. The priest left a cross in the hallway and told her always to leave it there, never to remove it or the haunting would start again.

STRATFORD-UPON-AVON

If the ghost of Shakespeare ever visited Stratford he would still be able to find his way around.

The street pattern - three roads parallel to the river and three streets crossing at right angles - is still there, laid out by the Bishop of Worcester as long ago as the thirteenth century. Many of the buildings, too, are still standing: the birthplace, Quiney house (the home of his daughter, Judith) and the Guild Chapel where he unwillingly crept to school. The two main landmarks remain intact despite some alterations. Clopton Bridge was widened and shortened, and the timber spire of Holy Trinity was replaced by a stone one.

But one house which Shakespeare's ghost wouldn't find is his own, New Place, which he bought in 1596 and lived in for the last six years of his life. It was built by the Clopton family and must have been one of the most imposing houses in Stratford. In 1756 it was sold to the Rev Francis Gastrell who eventually demolished it, apparently after a quarrel about the assessment of rates. Understandably, he was forced to leave the town 'amidst the rages and curses of the inhabitants'. The site of New Place has been bought by the Birthplace Trust and laid out as a garden.

Stratford has been a Shakespearean shrine for only the last 150 years but it was an important town in its own right for much longer than that. From the sixteenth to eighteenth centuries it was well-known for the skill of its weavers and for the manufacture of gloves, collars and other small items - Shakespeare's father is thought to have been a glover, woolstapler and agricultural merchant. Medieval Stratford was famous for its market: horses and cattle were driven long distances for sale there; and earlier still it was a Roman settlement with a ford where the Avon ran across the Roman road (Stratford deriving from 'street ford')

Shakespeare was a great enthusiast of the local ale and his ghost would no doubt be delighted to find many of his old haunts still in existence. Only a few yards from the site of New Place, for example, is The Falcon Hotel. Shakespeare, like present-day visitors, must have walked along its gleaming flagstones and through the half-darkness of its long, narrow entrance hall.

The Falcon dates from the late fifteenth century. In Shakespeare's time it was still one dwelling house but for three hundred years, until the beginning of this century, it was divided into three separate houses - 1, 2 and 3 Chapel Street. Number 1 was probably always used as an inn, but numbers 2 and 3, for most of the last century, appear to have been turned into a school.

In room 307, on the first floor, lurks a ghost. No-one has any idea of its identity but one thing is certain: since it is female it cannot be the spirit of Shakespeare! The history of The Falcon, as far as it is known, has been trouble-free, without any suicides or murders which could have left an impression on time.

The manager, Mr Denis Woodhams, describes his ghostly resident.

It always appears at exactly 4.30 am. First of all the room goes very cold. I have slept in the room - I haven't seen the ghost but I have experienced the sudden chill. It's very strange. My wife has slept in the room too; she hasn't seen the ghost either, but whenever she sleeps in there she has very vivid dreams. I particularly remember one Christmas morning about five years ago, when my son had just taken over the Arrow Mill, that she dreamt it had burned down.

Then, according to those who *have* seen it, a white female form appears to be sitting on the bed. This has happened four times in the twelve years I have been here. I was told about it when I arrived, but as I don't believe in ghosts I didn't think much about it. The room is a double one and contains a four-poster bed, so I always let it to married couples; and the pattern is the same each time: the wife wakes up, sees the ghost, lets out a yell and rouses her husband. It's always the woman who sees the ghost, never the man. The ghost is apparently only there for a few seconds and has gone by the time the husband has his eyes open properly.

They tell me that the apparition is always sitting on the bed and is without colour, so that it appears to be white from head to toe. She has long hair and a nightdress or long gown which would probably reach the floor. She's quite clearly defined so that those who have seen her reckon her to be in her early thirties.

On all four occasions when the ghost has been seen, the residents have come down to the reception desk the following morning and, with expressions of disbelief, have confided: 'I had a peculiar experience last night ... '

Clopton House

Of all the great houses in England, the history of Clopton House must surely rank amongst the most tragic. It is a story that has inspired both Shakespeare and Edgar Allen Poe and many lesser writers in between; for here a young girl was buried alive and another committed suicide; and in this house a priest was murdered while another became fatally involved in the Gunpowder Plot.

The Clopton family was at its height in the fifteenth century. By 1492, Sir Hugh Clopton held one of the most important offices of the time, Lord Mayor of London, having already endeared himself to the people of Stratford by building the town's bridge across the Avon.

The following century witnessed the most horrific incident in the family's history. It concerned one of the daughters of the house, Charlotte, a young girl noted for her beauty and 'sweet disposition', who in 1564, was one of the first victims of the plague in Stratford. As soon as she died she was interred with great haste in the family vault at Holy Trinity Church, so that the disease would not have time to spread. Only a few days later the plague claimed a second member of the Clopton family, Charlotte's mother. The vault was duly reopened and a dreadful sight met the eyes of the mourners. Charlotte's coffin was open and empty and the dead girl was propped against a wall of the vault. When she was buried she had evidently only been comatosed. She must have recovered to find herself in the coffin, managed to force her way out, but found herself sealed in the vault. She had died from starvation, in her anguish biting into her shoulder. The horror of this story inspired Shakespeare to write his *Romeo and Juliet* and Edgar Allen Poe to write his macabre novel *The Fall of the House of Usher*.

The ghost of a pretty young girl has been seen in the house a number of times, particularly in Charlotte's old bedroom. Some of those who have seen the ghost describe it as having a mass of fair hair which is tied back before it falls on the shoulders in ringlets. This corresponds to a portrait of Charlotte which hung in her bedroom until the 1850's. Evidently, the spirit of the poor young girl sometimes returns to the house where she was so happy.

The sixteenth century witnessed another tragedy, that of Margaret Clopton, who drowned herself in a well behind the house because her father refused to allow her to marry the man she loved.

Shakespeare (a regular visitor to the house where he set part of *The Taming of the Shrew*) is thought to have based Ophelia on Margaret, although Ophelia, more poetically, drowned in a brook.

> *There, on the pendant boughs her coronet weeds*
> *Clambering to hang, an envious sliver broke;*
> *When down her weedy trophies and herself*
> *Fell in the weeping brook.*

Margaret's ghost has been seen after nightfall many times throughout the centuries, wandering sadly round the site of the well and through the house.

Like many other aristocratic families in this area, the Cloptons remained staunchly Catholic during the religious persecutions of Elizabeth I and James I, a loyalty which resulted in the tragedies of the next century.

A room in the attic was used as an oratory and apparently a priest was in hiding there. He was discovered and murdered, then his body was dragged along the landing and thrown out through a window into the moat. It left a thin, dark bloodstain which can never be removed. His ghost has been seen in the attic on many occasions.

The final unfortunate character was Ambrose Rokewood or Rookwood, to whom the house was let in 1604. A quiet, pious man, his friendship with Catesby led him to become involved in the Gunpowder Plot of 5 November 1605, which went so disastrously wrong.

Clopton House remained in the Clopton family until 1873. In 1932 it was purchased by the Beecham family and became, for many years, the home of Lady Beechem, wife of the great conductor, Sir Thomas. The house has now been divided into private apartments.

Atherstone-on-Stour

Jill Brown, who describes herself as a very ordinary thirty-one year old wife and mother of three small children, has experienced three ghosts. She says, 'I was astonished to find that many of my friends, acquaintances and relatives also had had similar experiences but because of the fear of ridicule and disbelief thought it best to say nothing'.

Jill was only twelve when she experienced her first ghost, a few hours after her mother had tragically died from leukaemia.

> I took myself off across the fields for a walk alone. I had not gone far when I became distinctly aware of her presence walking beside me. She was holding my hand, assuring me she was still with me, and that I was not to worry, everything would be all right. I would have been only too happy to have stayed with her forever, but my father came looking for me with my brothers and my mum then left me.

Jill saw her second ghost a few years ago when living at her previous home.

> I was often aware of a black cat in the house, usually in the downstairs rooms. I own two cats myself and one of these is black and called Mick. But this ghost cat, who looked very real and solid, would often get mixed up with Mick. He would curl up on the settee in the evening looking exactly like Mick; but when at bedtime I asked my husband if he was going to put Mick out, he would often tell me he was already out - and on looking again, sure enough, the cat would be gone. Often, whilst working in the kitchen I would feel an animal brush around my legs, but when I looked down there would be nothing there.

This 'spirit' cat was seen by other people, including Jill's husband. Jill's third ghost made an appearance in the same house.

> I awoke one night to find a lady standing by the far corner of the bed. She was very solid and was wearing long skirts, an apron and a scullery cap; and in her hands she held a silver tea tray. I knew that she was as aware of me as I was of her. She walked up my husband's bedside cabinet as if to serve tea, then returned to the foot of the bed. She moved round the bed and started to walk towards me but I panicked and called my husband's name. When he awoke she disappeared. I have no idea who she was.

Jill is compiling a book of personal sightings 'to reassure others that they are not alone'. She also runs a self-help group for those who feel that they would like to talk about their experiences.

Hillborough

> *Piping Pebworth, dancing Marston,*
> *Haunted Hillborough, and hungry Grafton;*
> *With dodging Exhall, papist Wixford;*
> *Beggarly Broom, and drunken Bidford.*

So Shakespeare described eight villages clustered around the Avon valley just below Stratford.

But why, in a time when folklore and superstition were a part of everyday life, was Hillborough singled out as being haunted? Two ancient legends were probably sufficient to keep the ladies indoors in the evening. A phantom carriage and pair occasionally drives along Hillborough Lane while, in a nearby field, a lady clothed in white makes an appearance accompanied by a white stag.

Since Shakespeare's time Hillborough has acquired two other ghosts. On dark nights, blood-curdling screams are said to echo round the village. These belong to a local landowner who converted the villagers' cultivated plots into grazing for his sheep, causing much hardship. The villagers decided to administer their own justice and stoned him to death.

Down the centuries reports of husbands murdering their wives occur with some regularity (see Arrow Mill). On Good Friday in 1801 a Mr Palmer was hanged for this offence on the gibbet that stood in a nearby field - afterwards known as 'Palmer's Piece'. In those days, the body was usually left on display for some time to deter others. When Palmer's body was eventually removed, his spirit continued to haunt the area.

Shottery

Shottery is a place of pilgrimage for Shakespearean enthusiasts as it was in a cottage there that Shakespeare's wife, Anne Hathaway, was born.

Shottery lies on the western edge of Stratford, bordering the A422 Roman Road. Occasionally the pounding of hooves can be heard late at night along this road out of Stratford, although nothing is visible.

During the early 1980s a house in Hathaway Lane was haunted by a poltergeist. Objects were removed for a day or two, then replaced exactly where they had been. When the occupiers were away on holiday antique clocks were mysteriously rewound and found to be still working on their return.

Snitterfield

An anecdote about a UFO is really outside the scope of a book of ghost stories but there are two reasons for including this one: first, the *William Avery Memorial Volumes* (upon which this collection is based) recorded all paranormal phenomena, and secondly, it's a fascinating story. It comes from Snitterfield, a tiny ancient rural village on high ground approximately three miles north of Stratford. From 1668-1830 a great house stood there, built by the widow of Sir Stephen Hales. A mile away is Bearley where a powerful GPO short-wave transmitting and receiving station was built just after the Second World War and only recently dismantled.

In 1968 a schoolmaster living in Snitterfield had a most unusual experience. Fortunately, he had the presence of mind to record it in detail and his account is reproduced below.

The night of 3rd/4th August 1968 was, to most people in Britain, just an ordinary night with a slight wind blowing West to East across the country and with a low cloud-base blotting out the stars.

To me, however, unlike the other 50-odd million Britons, it was something truly dramatic and a night that I remember with considerable foreboding.

To begin at the beginning:

I joined my sleeping wife late on at about 11.30 pm on Saturday 3rd August, after walking through the house to ensure that our four young children had settled comfortably. Having completed this nightly ritual I went to look out of the mullioned window of our house which is situated in the heart of Shakespeare's England in the centre of the village of Snitterfield, three miles North of Stratford-upon-Avon, a village incidentally which was the home of the poet's father, who once farmed the area. These environs the Bard must have known intimately as a boy.

Before getting into bed, I pulled aside the curtain and peered out over the lawn, pausing long enough to notice the glow of street lighting reflected from the brooding clouds over Stratford to the South.

I must have fallen asleep normally, but I recall having the most vivid dream in which a person unknown to me was seated on a chair in a chamber-like compartment a short distance away, directing a powerful beam of light down towards me.

Suddenly, I awoke in a heavy sweat: at this instance I experienced something more frightening and even more horrific than the dream self.

Wide awake now, and with a reality more empirical than a road accident in the middle of a city at noon, I realised there WAS something out there, seemingly just beyond the open window with its curtain stirring gently in the breeze!

My body was held completely rigid and I was unable to move, apart from being free to manipulate my head from side to side. To convince myself that I was no longer dreaming, I made a point of noticing the strange way in which the curtains were blowing into the room, and I was also able to note the exact time on the illuminated face of my watch - '2.45 am'.

Without any warning I was suddenly gripped by the most intense discomfort - a highly-pitched but hardly audible oscillation caused such an acute pain within my head. I wanted to scream! My body was, however, so helpless, my vocal chords would just not function; mesmerised and perspiring heavily I stared beyond the window. I saw nothing unusual - yet from just beyond came a soft, strange, 'swishing' sound of what might have been a helicopter's blades rotating - but there was no engine-noise whatsoever! An unlikely situation indeed! This sound, superimposed on the excruciating high-frequency range vibrations, produced the most weird phenomenon imaginable.

I have read of high-range sound vibrations, beyond the range of human hearing, being produced by jet aircraft which disturb grazing cattle, causing them to stampede, and I am now convinced that this is the sort of thing I was experiencing at that terrifying moment. But, what was the cause, at that particular instance, of a combination of electronic oscillation and engine-less blade swishing? I believe that I was transfixed for quite two minutes in a magnetic force field! Again, what was the connection between my graphic dream that immediately preceded this experience, and the traumatic experience itself? Were my mind and my hearing especially hypersensitive at 2.45 am, on 4th August 1968? (I was trained as a musician and obtained an ARCM diploma with its demands for aural perception of the highest intensity).

After the two minutes, both the noise and the physical effect faded and my head was released from the severe grip of the force-field or whatever the influence was; and thus, dripping all over with perspiration, and with understandable palpitations, I examined the whole house from top to bottom. Creeping from room to room, I observed all four children soundly asleep, as was my wife, who had slept undisturbed through it all.

For the remainder of the night I lay awake, puzzled and frightened. I was accustomed to odd nocturnal sounds, living as I did in an old country house with four children, for I had on many occasions been disturbed by such things as bats moving under the rafters; nesting birds beneath the eaves; romantic hedgehogs snuffling in the bushes; the sudden cry of a dreaming child - but this was in a quite different category!

I hardly dare admit that I received a solicitous look from my wife over breakfast when I said that I had heard a UFO in the night!

From the Sunday we were away from Snitterfield until the end of the week, but during that time I was unable to get the memory of this incomprehensible encounter out of my mind; in fact I mentioned the matter with great seriousness to relatives living in Aylesbury and Dunstable.

On arriving home on the Friday I found myself, whilst casually thumbing through the pages of the *Stratford-upon-Avon Herald* of 9th August, confronted with a report on page 11: 'Unidentified Flying Object Observed Over Leamington Spa'. This town is six miles from Snitterfield! Even more amazing, the Leamington sighting was only five hours or so before the Snitterfield incident. There were also, according to the paper, reports of nurses at Shirley, near Birmingham, having seen 'Flying Saucers' on the previous Thursday.

My fascination at this juncture knew no bounds for I was convinced there was some link between the visual and auditory manifestations and I immediately contacted the British Association for Research into Unidentified Flying Objects. The very next day a representative came to see me and took a statement and, after two hours of conversation, he postulated the view that there was most certainly a connection between the two. This gentleman told me that Coventry sightings had been reported about the same time.

It was explained to me that he thought at that moment, early on the Sunday morning, my mind was for some reason in a highly receptive state and I had unwittingly 'tuned-in' to a vehicle from beyond our galaxy! Furthermore, whereas sightings of strange occurrences in the skies all over the world are common, auditory contacts are very rare and combined contacts extremely so. (There was nevertheless a famous occasion in recent years when two policemen in Devon were subjected to the latter).

I should say that at Bearley, a village one mile west of Snitterfield, there is one of the most powerful short-wave radio receiving stations in the world. This is on a disused airfield which is festooned with lofty aerials, and quite possibly the homing point for the 'visitors' of 4th August.

A few days after this, I was asked to contact a retired Royal Air Force Wing Commander who lived in Loxley Road, Stratford-upon-Avon, because I was told he would be interested in my story. Calling one afternoon, I had to wait in his lounge where there was time to notice framed photographs of the Wing Commander in his service days. Here was a man with thirty years of flying in the Air Force who, in spite of his airborne career, had his feet, metaphorically speaking, 'very firmly on the ground'.

It transpired during the interview over tea, that the ex-RAF pilot had himself observed UFOs performing - in his own words: 'Right angle turns at 2,000 miles per hour over Salisbury Plain in the early 1950s'. Two other observers were with him at the time when he did his trigonometry to calculate the speed of what he was seeing.

From a man who had spent much of his life flying aeroplanes and from one who claimed to know the heavens and all the constellations like the back of his hand, it was certainly dramatic to hear him say at the end of our discussion: 'The noise you heard; the physical discomfort you endured; the sightings some hours before 4th August, were all linked simply because - for a brief moment in eternity - a flying saucer hovered at no great height over your house in Snitterfield'.

Wellesbourne, Walton Hall Hotel

Wellesbourne lies four miles east of Stratford. Now a quiet rural village, it was virtually the capital of the Midlands in Anglo-Saxon times, when the Mercian Council was held there regularly.

Wellesbourne comprises two villages divided by the river Dene, Wellesbourne Hastings to the north-east and Wellesbourne Mountford to the south-west, both named after families influential during the middle ages. Walton Hall is situated on the road between Wellesbourne Mountford and Pillerton Priors. Although it might look medieval the hall was built between 1858 and 1862 by G G Scott, the well-known Victorian architect.

A ghost of a young man appears once every few years in the library, the cocktail bar and room 117. Lady Hamilton, who owns the Walton estate, gives this description of the last known sighting:

When the house was a hotel, the manager asked me if I would talk to a guest who was convinced she had seen a ghost - she was acknowledged to be a bit 'psychic'. She and her husband were staying in a room to the left of the front courtyard - and she told me that she woke to find a young man looking down at her. She didn't feel frightened but woke her husband, whereupon the figure disappeared. The young man was fair-haired and, as we have a portrait of my husband's grandfather and he was fair-haired, I asked her to come and look to see if he resembled the 'ghost' she'd seen - unfortunately, he didn't. I told the lady that the fair young man could have been a footman, as the room she stayed in was part of the servants' wing.

People who have seen ghosts have always told me that the apparition seemed perfectly ordinary - it was only when they noticed that they were, say, wearing period clothes that it was apparent they were ghostly beings. My husband, when he produced 'Hamlet', put this into practice by making the ghost of Hamlet's father appear as an ordinary person - no strange lights, ominous music, floating mist or ghostly garments - and the effect was amazing.

Ghostly Gossip

A white horse is said to gallop across the front lawns once every five years on 9 October. The traditional explanation is that one of the ladies of the house was having an affair with a prince. Her husband arrived home unexpectedly one day and her aristocratic lover managed to escape but not before her husband had taken a few pot shots in his direction, killing the prince's white horse. The lady later gave birth to a mentally subnormal boy who was locked away in the west wing.

Lady Hamilton writes that this story is not altogether accurate and comments:

> The legend concerns the first Lady Mordaunt. She had a daughter (by Sir Charles) who was mentally normal and grew up to be a great beauty. It was the second Lady Mordaunt who had five daughters and a mentally deficient son who died in his thirties.

STUDLEY

About 150 years ago, Tom's Town in Studley had the reputation of being the most haunted place in the Redditch area, 'never without some ghost or other'!

The line of the old Roman Icknield Street (now the A435) passes through the centre of the village. Studley is old enough to be listed in the Domesday book and evidence of its antiquity can be seen in St Mary's Church, where a small decorated doorway and a stone carving of the lamb and the cross date back to Norman times.

For the last three centuries, Studley has been famous for its springs and needles which culminated in the giant Needle Industries Group Limited, formed in 1931.

Watts Road

The ghosts of Tom's Town have long since disappeared but a young couple who recently moved into nearby Watts Road have been puzzled by strange occurrences in their home. The house is about thirty years old and has been thoroughly modernised by the young husband. Over a period of twelve months there have been three curious incidents. The husband tells the story.

The first thing which happened, towards the end of 1990, was the most weird. We have a dried-flower arrangement in our bedroom and we arrived home from work one evening to find it spread round the bedroom, just as if someone had thrown it round the place. This was so strange that I determined to find out what had caused it. I replaced the flowers and left the door open to recreate any draught; but nothing happened. Although we knew the window had been closed we tried opening it just to see if that would affect anything but, again, nothing happened. I never found any explanation for this.

Early in 1991 I was working on a loft conversion and I know without any doubt that when I went out of that loft for a cup of coffee I turned the radio off. Yet when I went back upstairs ten minutes later the radio had been turned on again.

About the same time, I was about to go into the bathroom one evening when the bathroom door gave slightly but slammed shut again and wouldn't open. I tried a second time and the same thing happened. It was just as if someone was holding the door from the other side. A few minutes later it opened without any difficulty.

I'm not suggesting that we have a ghost or anything. There's probably an explanation for these incidents, but they were certainly very weird.

Studley Castle

The impressive mock-medieval towers and turrets of Studley Castle is now the home of the Marketing Institute of the Rover Group who have renovated and restored it with affection and pride.

Brenda Hunting, Manager of Administration & Facilities, gives a brief history of the castle and describes its ghost:

This building is known as Studley Castle but the original castle stood about half-a-mile away, near the parish church; there is now nothing left of that except a few portions of the moat. This place, I am told, was built in 1833 by Sir Francis Holyoak who, rumour has it, had it erected within one year and one day for a bet. He was a young man and in the same year he married. His wife was supposed to have had an affair with one of the estate workers and I presume she became pregnant. Her husband threw the baby out of a window into the pool (which is still there, to the right of the drive as you go away from the house) and she rushed into the pool to save her baby and was drowned. The legend is that this distraught mother is the Grey Lady who haunts Studley Castle.

The chambermaids are adamant that there is a 'something'; quite frequently they have felt their shoulders brushed as if a person were walking past. Other people have said that they sense the lady's spirit from the smell of lavender in certain bedrooms.

The presence of the Grey Lady is felt particularly in the east wing, which was derelict until nine years ago when we converted it into ninety-seven bedrooms. The smell of lavender is quite strong here and as the windows are often closed, it could not have come in from outside. As you walk through you sense that there is something and yet you're not scared; you merely feel as if there is a sad spirit present. I often come here late at night in the dark and I only bother to put one light on. I don't feel afraid at all.

Studley Castle was an Agricultural College for Ladies until 1969 and former students often return for reunions. The ladies, anywhere between forty to ninety years of age, frequently talk about the ghost. They are convinced there is something, that the place is haunted.

Many of our directors and overseas delegates who come here comment on the feeling of peace and contentment, on the quiet relaxed atmosphere which enables them to get a lot of work done.

Studley Priory

A priory existed at Studley for almost three hundred years on the west bank of the river Arrow, not quite half a mile north-west of the parish church. It was dissolved in 1536 and the few existing remains were incorporated into Chapel Farm.

A thirteenth-century coffin lid was found on the priory site in 1931 and is now on display in the parish church. In the centre is a cross entwined with foliage and an inscription runs along two edges.

Arthur Daniels, who lives in Studley and is a keen amateur historian, writes:

> In 1981, when the Priory remains were disturbed by drain-laying, I collected a bag full of human bones from the spoil-heaps - in the same spot the coffin lid was found! The occupiers of the eventually-built barn conversions were made uncomfortable by the noise of shuffling feet at dead of night. They sold up and moved out. The noise has never been heard since.

From Old Published Reports

Sixty years ago the Priory at Studley had its ghost, a white shadowy figure that haunted one of the upper rooms of the house. This room contained besides other lumber a suit of mail and a helmet or two, since removed by Mr. Cooper, of Henley, (steward to the proprietor of the Priory estate), (and given to) a Mr.Knight, Mr. Cooper probably thinking that armour was more suitable for a knight than a farmer.

The room was the bedroom of James Kelly, the carter, and a boy, Joseph, who helped in farm work. It seems that both were new comers, engaged at the last Studley Mop. On their retiring to rest they surveyed the old helmets, &c., and went to bed. About midnight, however, a lumbering sound as of a coffin being dragged upstairs, awoke them; then came the clanking of chains, and they were aware before them of a shadowy, white figure moving round their bed. How long the vision tarried I am not informed, but Kelly on the next night took up a pitchfork and placed it at his bed's head, and both waited for the ghost.

In due time the thing appeared, heralding its coming by the lumbering noise before mentioned, and Kelly struck at the shadowy form bravely with his pitchfork, but the weapon of course could not hurt a disembodied being, but passed clean through it without even discomposing the phantom in the least. My informant could not say how many nights the man and boy bore the sight of this awful presence, but

they were so harassed by the thing that they determined to leave. Joseph
—- went to the needles and Kelly, who had saved money, took a small
farm at Middletown.

J M Woodward

Tom's Town (spelt Tomes's Town in old records) and Gunner's Lane

We have to thank the anonymous author of the next two stories
for the fascinating glimpse of the day-to-day life of the working
people in Studley just over a hundred years ago.

At Studley my informant states that he had met with two instances
of the phantoms of living persons appearing to him shortly before those
persons died. There was at Studley a highly respectable family of the
name of Hay, consisting of the mother and two daughters. The latter
were dressmakers and lived nearly opposite the "Duke of Marlborough,"
while the mother lived in her own cottage at Tomes's Town, a locality in
which ghosts were plentiful 50 years ago; in short, Tomes's Town then
was never without some ghost or other. It would be about that time
when my neighbour, then a boy of sixteen, hearing that there was a
ghost to be seen (though he cannot now remember amongst so many
what particular one was then in vogue) determined to take a walk at
night, and prove the truth or falseness of the current rumour.
Accordingly, he went round Squire Chambers's property and along
Gunner's Lane, which, leading in the direction of the churchyard, was no
doubt a likely road for a ghost given to walking to take. He did not
however light upon anything supernatural there, and so passed through
Gunner's Lane clap-gate into the high road and walked towards Studley.
At this time the moon shone brightly and he saw before him the well-
known figure of Mrs Hay. She had patten clogs on her feet, and he could
distinctly hear the ring of the pattens upon the road. He hastened to
overtake the old lady, whom he knew well, and as he went by her said,
"How are you, Mrs Hay?". There was no reply. He turned round and Mrs
Hay had vanished, patten-clogs and all! Astonished at this strange
occurrence he hastened homeward and told a friend what he had seen,
and in a few days the old lady (Mrs Hay) vanished for ever from her own
little cottage at Tomes's Town and occupied her present tenement in
Studley churchyard.

Another hallucination with a similar result happened by daylight, on a beautiful sunny Sunday morning. My neighbour was then but young, and lay in bed after the rest of the household had gone down stairs. "I was not asleep or dozing, but wide awake," says he, "when I saw my brother-in-law, a needle pointer, enter the room in his working dress of corduroy. He passed by my bedside and vanished through the closed window of the room. I called my mother and told her what I had seen. She replied that I must have been mistaken, but my brother-in-law died the week after, nevertheless."

(Both of these old records, one referring to Studley Priory and the other to Tom's Town and Gunner's Lane, came from the William Avery Memorial Volumes*)*

ULLENHALL

Barrells Hall

Barrells Hall was owned by the Knight family from the sixteenth century up until 1924. Robert Knight who became the owner in 1730 married Henrietta St John, a member of an old and honourable family. They were not seen very often at Barrells Hall as most of their time was spent in the fashionable society of London and Bath.

There was some surprise when, after nine years of marriage, Robert accused his wife of an illicit relationship with their children's tutor. Poor Henrietta protested her innocence but was nevertheless banished to Barrells Hall, never to see her children again, and not permitted to leave England or travel within twenty miles of London or Bath. Robert Knight prospered at court and became Baron Luxborough and later, Viscount Barrells and Earl of Catherlough. Henrietta preferred to be known simply as Lady Luxborough.

It gives the historian some satisfaction to record that, while the Earl of Catherlough has passed into obscurity, the name of his banished wife is remembered. She gathered together a social circle who, like herself, were artistic, intelligent, creative and witty, among them William Shenstone, William Somervile and Richard Jago. The correspondence between members of this circle sheds great light on the day-to-day life of the eighteenth-century upper class.

William Shenstone and Lady Luxborough were keen gardeners and they competed to see who could create the most beautiful environment. Sadly, very little of her garden at Barrells Hall remains. The bowling green, the hermitage, the ha-ha, the statues and urns have all vanished. The avenues of trees are overgrown and almost impassable. The lake and the lily ponds have formed into a single natural pool.

A fire in 1933 destroyed most of the house which has become a picturesque ruin - complete with ghost; for the apparition of a lady is said to have been seen a number of times. In 1979 a young girl was playing among the ruins with a group of friends when she looked up and saw a beautiful lady in an exquisite, long blue dress at the top of a flight of ruinous stairs.

The stables of Barrells Hall have been converted into a dwelling and Miss Gillian Hyde now lives there. She says that, although she has never seen the ghost of Lady Luxborough, various curious incidents have occurred.

My bedsitter is the old tack room and even when the doors are closed I sometimes feel a draught, just as if someone has walked past. One day, my young nephew and I were sitting here and a picture, which I kept between the pages of a book on my shelves, flew out as if it had been pushed from the binding. I have been woken up in the night by someone sitting on my bed, the last time about twelve months ago. It sits down, gets up then sits down again. Yet there's no-one there. I've also heard a noise as if someone were trying to get out of the bathroom - but its empty.

I'm not at all frightened. There is a very happy atmosphere here. After all, Lady Luxborough lived here for twenty years and loved this house and its garden. The anemonies are out at the moment, masses of them. They were Lady Luxborough's favourite flower and when I walk through the gardens I feel I'm very close to her. Sometimes I can smell her perfume - fresh old-fashioned lavender water. Other people have noticed it too. My niece Rachel was here the other day and asked me what the smell was. The first time I smelt it was in the holly walk one Sunday, just before lunch, a time when Lady Luxborough would have been taking a stroll there.

However, a few years ago there was one incident which terrified me. One day I had asked the gardener to shut the chickens up, but late evening I decided to check as the hounds were going to be out the next day. As I was coming back to the corner not far from the stables I was certain that someone was behind me. I turned round to look but the night was dark and misty. I'm not a nervous person but that feeling was so strong it really frightened me. My hair stood on end, I lengthened my stride and when I got to the bottom of the path I started to run. My friend, Brian, saw me and said 'What's up with you, you're as white as a sheet?'. I explained what had happened and he said that on a couple of occasions he had felt something behind him, too but decided not to say anything in case I was alarmed.

That's the only time I have been frightened. I love living here and I'm very happy.

(Please note that Barrells Hall is private property and trespassers are prosecuted)

UPPER BENTLEY

Norgrove Court

Maudie Ellis describes Norgrove Court perfectly in *The Squire of Bentley:*

> Norgrove was the home of the Cookes family who at one time owned the whole of Feckenham Forest, including Bentley Heath and Tardebigge. It is considered to be one of the very first houses ever built with bricks, everyone of which was hand-made. The architecture is very wonderful and stands today as of yore, an enormous house with beautiful mullioned windows and possessing massive octagonal chimneys beyond description. Its historic interest (including its ghost and its traditions) have preserved through the centuries an atmosphere of the days of chivalry in which Norgrove played its noble part.

Mr and Mrs Sinclair have lived in the house since 1968. Mrs Sinclair describes the hauntings.

> We have two manifestations: a lady dressed in black and a phenomenon which only visitors staying in the house are supposed to hear - the sounds of revelry, of horses arriving, of everything going quiet, as though a message has been brought, and then of the horses galloping away.
>
> Once, we had a French boy staying. One morning, he came downstairs at about 5.30. I asked him why he had got up so early, as he wasn't normally an early riser. He said 'You came in and told me to get up. You were wearing a long black dressing gown'. Of course, I hadn't been anywhere near his room.
>
> This house isn't spooky at all. It has large, light rooms and there are no dark passages. On the whole, we haven't come across anything - except for what could be perhaps a poltergeist. It might be something to do with with our youngest son, William. Nothing happened until he was about eighteen months old (I have heard that poltergeists are connected with young children); but then various incidents began to occur. Things are always disappearing, for example, as they do in any family and I always think it's our own fault. But once the very efficient lady who does some typing for my husband put a pile of papers by the typewriter and they disappeared.
>
> More startling, I was once in the kitchen when a biro flew through the air and hit me on the cheek; another time I heard a noise in the kitchen

and when I went to investigate I found a pile of ice in the sink. Where the ice had come from I don't know; it was the middle of summer.

One evening, I was upstairs and my husband and son were sitting in our small sitting room which is halfway up the stairs. I was upstairs. We have a gramophone in the dining room which has a brush for cleaning the records and my husband saw this brush fly across the hall. He came up to ask me if I had thrown the brush. I said that of course I hadn't.

Old Published Reports

The following is another excerpt from *The Squire of Bentley*

That Norgrove is haunted and that its ghosts belong to a period before its restoration in 1649 adds still further interest to its history in these days of psychic research. Historic ghosts they are too, and ghostly happenings in the presence of the astral of a charming lady are undoubtedly felt and seen in Norgrove ... In recent years these Norgrove spirits and spirit sounds have appeared to and been heard by unsuspecting people who had never even heard of the existence of either, and who, therefore, had no anticipation or imagination quickened. In some cases they were strangers to the house and its traditions, and in others, even if they knew all the facts ... they were sceptical and unafraid. Many of these have seen and heard from the Norgrove spirits during the last four years and have gone away not doubting but confirmed believers.

In 1906 Norgrove underwent many improvements within its walls, for "The Squire" redecorated all the principal rooms to the north and west for her eldest son Hugh when he married in 1907 ...

All this gave the young couple much pleasure and interest to their home and the fact that they lived in a haunted house only added romance to their new abode, for they felt, as we all did, that Norgrove ghosts have their charm. One evening when Hugh was standing at the drawing-room door he distinctly saw "the lady" gracefully ascending the old oak staircase. The farm bailiffs and their families who lived there during "The Squire's" reign also heard ghostly strangers in the house, and the banging of doors that were known to be bolted and barred, and learnt to take but little notice of them. At another time, a young farm pupil, a lad hitherto of no fears, also saw the lady. During a Spring clean the bailiff's wife changed his quarters from the east side of the house to one of the large guest rooms on the west. In the night he awoke feeling a presence in the room and lighting his candle he saw her figure for a second standing in the centre of the room, but she immediately glided away and passed transparently through the closed doors. This experience so alarmed the young man that another room had to be provided for him.

And again, there is the story of a disturbed night owing to these same ghostly happenings, as experienced by one of these unsuspecting people, a friend of the bailiff from the west country. She was sleeping in the principal guest room and was awakened suddenly by sounds that at first conveyed the impression of a gathering and lighthearted revelry. (No doubt the ground floor at Norgrove was originally one large banqueting hall and the staircase as it stands today, unaltered for generations, is wide enough for four persons to walk abreast.) She distinctly heard the clanking of armour and the rustle of silk, together with voices and dancing feet. Suddenly came the sound of horses' feet galloping in the distance; nearer and nearer they came, until they drew up below her very window! There was a sudden quiet. Then followed commotion: dancing feet altered to disordered, hasty and heavy footfalls; anxious voices and shouts of men, intermixed with an occasional feminine voice, expressing sensitive anxiety. Again there came a lull, and then she heard horses galloping away at the same furious pace at which they had arrived.

The bailiff had carefully never mentioned that Norgrove was haunted, so that in this case no fear of ghosts was present in her mind, nor had she any clue as to the period which she so graphically described. We felt that this particular night in July might have been the anniversary of some sudden summons - possibly a warning of approaching danger - that so hurriedly broke up the gathering. After this that room was usually given a miss in the month of July! It seems a pity that fear prevents most people from taking the chance again, and that even if there should be a listener, he lies petrified beneath the bedclothes instead of enjoying such a historic chapter in history.

(*From* The Squire of Bentley)

The common belief that the "red hand" on the shield of a baronet is the mark of Cain, and the tale that one of the Cookes family had murdered his groom and buried him under a tree at Norgrove, have jointly had their influence in locating a ghost in a wainsccotted chamber in the hall. Into this dark room it was said that no light could be carried, this being instantly put out by a supernatural blast of wind. No doubt had the matter been looked into at the it would have been found that the ghost was nothing more than a church mouse, or a leattern-bat, that, attracted by the light, flew towards it and put it out by its wings or the wind occasioned by them.

(*From* The William Avery Memorial Volumes)

WOOTTON WAWEN

Hanging on the wall of Wootton Wawen church is a copy of an Anglo-Saxon document dated about 725 AD, showing that the King of Mercia gave twenty hides of Wootton for the building of a monastery. Nobody knows what happened to the monastery, but it was probably destroyed by the Danes who swept across the county in 1016.

There was, of course, yet another invasion in 1066. By this time the church of St Peter's had been built (the three lower storeys of the tower are the original Anglo-Saxon). The Normans, apparently more civilised than the Danes, did not destroy the church but merely gave it, together with the village, to a relative of William the Conqueror who adopted the name of de Stafford. He in turn gave the church to the Benedictines, the "black monks" so called because of their black hood and gown. They believed not only in poverty, chastity and obedience but also in manual labour as a duty to God and man. The priory they built, situated between the church and the vicarage, has unfortunately completely disappeared. But one magnificent residence in the area has survived: Wootton Hall, a large stone Palladian building, dated 1687 although parts of it are Elizabethan.

Wootton Hall was once famous throughout England as the favourite haunt of the Prince of Wales (later George IV). In this lovely old house his romance with the widow Maria Ann Fitzherbert blossomed and flourished; here the couple spent their happiest days. They were married in 1785 but ten years later, while Maria was still alive, the king was persuaded in return for the settlement of his debts to marry Caroline of Brunswick. He attempted on his accession to the throne to divorce Caroline but there was such an outcry that he abandoned the idea.

Wootton Hall

The walls of Wootton Hall have witnessed passionate romance, murder and the burial (in the churchyard next door) of hundreds of plague victims. Small wonder that rumours of ghosts are plentiful. Even the historian, Mr W Cooper, describes two paranormal incidents at the hall. The present owners are Mr and Mrs Allen. Here Jacky talks about some of their ghosts:

I knew this house for many, many years before I married my husband and so I came to know all the ghost stories connected with it. The most interesting is the ghost of Mrs Fitzherbert, who had a passionate love affair with the Prince Regent. They spent a great deal of time here. I presume that there were many strong feelings and much dramatic suspense because she truly loved him. I would think that love is the strongest form of spiritual awareness. Many years ago, her ghost was seen outside the front of the house, then it disappeared through the closed front doors.

Some people, including my husband who is very down to earth, believe that they can smell Mrs Fitzherbert's perfume. I thought this was imagined until I experienced it myself. I never wake up early and very rarely feel immediately wide awake but on this gloriously sunny morning I woke up bright as a button. I sat up in bed, the sun streaming in, and I smelt a perfume just like Blue Grass. I was staying in the house temporarily so only had my Chanel with me; and my husband was going through his Old Spice stage. So I knew, since there was no-one else here, that it wasn't a perfume of ours. I went off to sleep again and woke up at the usual time; but the memory of that perfume has never left me. In fact, at that time I had never heard of Blue Grass. It was only later that I came across it and recognised it as Mrs Fitzherbert's perfume. I only ever smelt it once - a friend of mine has experienced it frequently - but it was such a fresh, natural perfume. Maria Fitzherbert was a very beautiful woman who liked to be natural; she did not like to be powdered and bewigged. When Gainsborough was commissioned to paint her portrait he refused to proceed because she would not wear all the regalia he thought appropriate.

When we were first married, my husband often smelt the perfume and would say, 'There's Mrs Fitz again!'. He once had a group of bankers and solicitors meeting here who all experienced the perfume and my husband said 'Oh, that's Mrs Fitz'.

My stepdaughter, who has a sombre and steady personality and is totally sceptical, has seen the Grey Lady. This ghost is sometimes confused with Mrs Fitzherbert's but she is entirely different. The Grey Lady manifests herself in a severe grey dress with grey hair tied back into a bun. My daughter was going upstairs with the dogs when they bristled and yapped. She looked up and saw a woman. She is supposed to have been a servant who worked here and had an affair with a member of the Smythe family who built the hall. Both of them mysteriously disappeared and when the dairy was pulled down the workmen found two skeletons, the one of a very tall man over six feet, the other of a very small woman whom we assume to be the Grey Lady.

We have other ghosts who have been seen by reliable and responsible people in the village and on the estate. Two hooded monks in dark robes walk down the drive and kneel and pray at the Coventry Piece (an unmarked area of the churchyard next to the drive). When Coventry was suffering from the plague they found it difficult to bury all the bodies so they had to use mass graves. We are in the diocese of Coventry so a pit was dug in the churchyard and the bodies buried there. The hooded monks are said to be praying for the Coventry Piece. Curiously, their faces are never seen and they manifest themselves in the daytime as well as the night. They were last seen early one morning about ten years ago.

Jacky Allen was invited to appear on a television programme about paranormal experiences. Further details are given under 'Comment' at the end of the book.

Old Published Reports

In his book *Wootton Wawen, Its History and Its Records*, W Cooper corroborates the story of the two skeletons found in the dairy and provides another ghost. He quotes Mr W F Tempest, tenant of Wootton Hall from 1860 to 1867, who tells how a servant named Betty Harris refused to go into the dairy at night because she said she could see the figure of a man sitting in the corner. A few years later, in 1861, when the dairy was pulled down, the skeleton of a man and a woman were found under the exact spot where she had seen the ghost! No-one knows their identity for certain but suspicions are that the first owner of the hall and his dairymaid were murdered and secretly buried there.

Mr Tempest also tells how his little fox terrier, which slept in his room, would sometimes jump onto his bed at night, trembling with fear.

The next tenant at the hall after Mr Tempest was a Mr Haycock 'who was much troubled with a spirit knocking at his door, and a friend staying with him had the same experience. The friend tried to open the door to see what it was, but the door was pulled to violently!'

Comment

Jacky Allen of Wootton Hall was invited, along with an Anglican minister and a medium, to take part in a television programme about people who have had paranormal experiences. When she began talking about her fondness for Mrs Fitzherbert, the minister was appalled, saying that every ghost was evil. When the programme was over he offered to exorcise Mrs Fitzherbert's ghost, saying that it would only remain friendly until Jacky put her trust in it, then it would manifest itself as evil. Jacky told him that she did not want the ghost exorcised.

What is the official Church of England attitude towards ghosts? The Venerable Frank Bentley, Archdeacon of Worcester comments:

> I believe the view of the minister as described ... to be a personal one, and not in any sense representative of the official view of the church. For a better understanding, may I suggest that you obtain a copy of *Deliverance* edited by Michael Perry on behalf of the Christian Exorcism Study Group, published by SPCK 1987 at £4.95. (Also Michael Perry's earlier book *Psychic Studies*, the Aquarian Press 1984 and 1986 is of interest).
>
> The first book has an interesting chapter on ghost and place memories, including a series of actual cases. Archdeacon Perry concludes that most cases are 'memories', not entities, and are neither good nor evil, though there are some place memories which are the result of deliberate sin, and these cases are a cause for special concern and action. There is also an excellent history of church attitudes.

Haunted Inns and Hotels

For those intrepid ghost hunters who would like to spend the night in a haunted building, the options are as follows:

The Falcon Hotel, Stratford, in room 307
The Old Rectory, Ipsley, near Redditch, in the old chapel room
The Arrow Mill, Arrow, near Alcester
The Bull's Head, Inkberrow, Worcester
Salford Hall Hotel, Abbots Salford, Warwickshire
(Murder weekends also available here)
The White Swan, Henley-in-Arden, in room 17.

Bibliography

ATKINS M *Haunted Warwickshire* (Robert Hale, 1981)
§ AUTHOR UNKNOWN *The Tragic Story of Salford Hall*
(Reprinted 1990)
BORD J & E *Ancient Mysteries of Britain* (Guild Publishing, 1986)
*CASE E *The Odour of Sanctity* (to be updated and reprinted shortly)
#COOPER W *Wootten Wawen, Its History and Its Records*
(J Whitehead, 1936)
#ELLIS M *The Squire of Bentley* (Blackwood, 1926)
#GWINNETT A *A History of Alcester* (Published privately, 1947)
#GWINNETT A *The Story of the Angel Inn,* Alcester
(Published privately, 1966)
LAND N *Victorian Workhouse* (Brewin Books, 1990)
PALMER R *The Folklore of Warwickshire* (Batsford, 1976)
PEARSON J *Jim's Book* (St Leonard's Church guide, Beoley, 1989)
SMITH B *Tales of Old Warwickshire* (Countryside Books, 1989)
WOODWARD J *The History of Bordesley Abbey* (1866)
Excerpts from the *Redditch Advertiser*.

The eight volumes of *The William Avery Memorial Papers* are in Redditch library and were collected between 1823 and William Avery's death in 1899. His friend, William Page, worked on the arrangement of the collection until 1906. The ghost stories are quoted from volume 1 and are cuttings from the *Redditch Indicator*.

§ Available from The Proprietor, Salford Hall Hotel, Abbots Salford, Warwickshire.
* Available from Mrs E Case, Red Rock, Brampford Speke, Exeter, Devon.
# Obtainable from the relevant local library.

Index

Page numbers in bold type refer to illustrations and their captions.